Saints and Sinners
in the
Early Church

Saints and Sinners in the Early Church

Differing and Conflicting Traditions
in the
First Six Centuries

W. H. C. Frend

Darton, Longman and Todd
London

First published in Great Britain in 1985 by
Darton, Longman and Todd Ltd
89 Lillie Road, London SW6 1UD

First published in 1985 by
Michael Glazier, Inc.
1723 Delaware Avenue
Wilmington DE 19806

ISBN 0 232 51663 4

British Library Cataloguing in Publication Data
Frend, W.H.C.
  Saints and sinners in the early church.
  1. Church history—Primitive and early church,
  ca. 30-600
  I. Title
  270.1   BR165

ISBN 0-232-51663-4

Printed and bound in Great Britain by
Anchor Brendon Ltd, Tiptree, Essex

Contents

Introduction

It is more than forty years since the late Canon G. L. Prestige gave his Bampton Lectures on the subject of *Fathers and Heretics in the Early Church*. This short sketch of the personalities and views of those who fell on one side or the other of the dividing line between orthodoxy and heresy has never been bettered. The aim of these 1981 Walter and Mary Tuohy lectures has been to research a little behind these ideas and substitute for orthodoxy and heresy that of gradually diverging and contrasting traditions in the early Church which resulted in the doctrinal and ecclesiastical controversies of the day, and to follow these through the lives of some of their leading representatives.

The author has had to be severely selective. Not everything can be said within the confines of six lectures. Thus, the Monarchians and Arius, who have attracted the attention of generations of able scholars, have been left out as have Ambrose and Priscillian,[1] while a new chapter on Pelagius (based upon a paper given in August 1976 at the University of South Africa) has been added. This has been done to maintain the continuity between the time of Donatus and that of Nestorius and to complete Augustine's contribution to Western theology through his long controversy

---

[1]In Ch. 2 discussion has centred on Basilides rather than Valentinus as representative Gnostics.

with Pelagius and Julian of Eclanum. I have also looked beyond Chalcedon (451) to the formation of the Monophysite Churches largely under the inspiration of the theology of Severus of Antioch.

I am very grateful to John Carroll University for its nomination to hold the Walter and Mary Tuohy Chair of Interreligious Studies for the Fall semester of 1981, and it is in the pleasant and cooperative atmosphere of the university that I have been able to prepare these lectures for publication.

I am very grateful to Mrs. Ellen Kelly for typing the manuscript.

W. H. C. Frend

1

One Lord, One Faith, One Baptism: The Ideal and the Reality

I start with two confessions. First, I have an instinctive sympathy for history's runners-up. In the history of Early Christianity, that includes those whose views never quite won acceptance, whose lives, like that of Julian of Eclanum, Augustine's opponent in the Pelagian controversy, ended in relative failure or who, like the Covenanters of the Dead Sea, failed to make their hoped-for impact on the destinies of mankind. In this book, I want to draw your attention to some examples and even to invite a few speculations on the "might-have-beens" of their time. What for instance would have happened had Pope Innocent (401-417) not condemned the Pelagians in 417 (just before he died) and so prevented Stoicism from playing the same significant role in western Christian thought that Platonism did in the east? Tertullian's quip, "Seneca saepe noster" (Seneca often ours [in sentiment])[1] might have prevailed. What would western theology in the Middle Ages have been like without the overhanging dreads resulting from the acceptance of predestination and what we now realise to have been the moral

---

[1] Tertullian, *De Anima*, 20, "sicut et Seneca saepe noster," ed. A. Reifferscheid, *Corpus Scriptorum Ecclesiasticorum Latinorum* (= *CSEL*) 20, 332.

taboos of Augustinian theology? Secondly, I believe that university professors are not dwellers in towers, ivory or otherwise, and that part of their duty is to place the results of their thought and experience at the disposal of their contemporaries for guidance in current problems. I wrote to the *London Times* on 30th January 1981 suggesting that there never was a time when Jesus' followers were truly united, and that the difference between "Nazarenes" in Jerusalem and "Christians" at Antioch as early as c. 39 A.D. marked the early emergence of an important difference of emphasis between Christians of Palestine and the Dispersion respectively. Should not this have some bearing on our ideas of Christian unity today?

So, if you put this two and two together, you will guess rightly that our study will have something to say about the schismatics and heretics of the early Church. In the second century these included the Alexandrian Gnostics, Basilides and the shipowner from Sinope on the Black Sea, Marcion. For the third century, we turn to Origen, one of the greatest thinkers of the early Church whose ideas inspired both heretics and orthodox in the Greek-speaking Church. Then we move to the west and examine the contributions made by Tertullian, Cyprian and Donatus to the ideal of the "gathered Church." For the classic Age of the Fathers, we have chosen Nestorius, the luckless archbishop of Constantinople (428-431) and at the other end of the Christological spectrum, Severus of Antioch (c. 467-538), who laid the foundations for the Monophysite churches in Syria, Egypt, Armenia and Ethiopia that survive today. These also contributed to the "pattern of Christian truth." There is light and shade in the history of Christianity. Ostensible failure is not always negative.

Indeed, if we take sometime around the year 600 A.D. as the final date for our study, we shall find that Christendom has already begun to assume the outlines of the pattern that we recognise today. In the west, the papacy has emerged as the focus of authority and organisation and the centre whence all mission to the heathen is directed. Germanic Arianism has been defeated, yet there remains in the background the legacy of schism and dualistic heresy which will emerge again to challenge the universalistic claims of the Catholic Church. In the east, the Roman version of these latter have never been accepted. The Pope was regarded as "archbishop of Old Rome," accorded a primacy of honour, but not jurisdiction over his brother minister, the archbishop of the capital of the empire, Constantinople, who in turn was senior to the patriarchs of Antioch, Jerusalem and Alexandria in communion with him. Those out of communion were also important. The Nestorians, now centred in Persia beyond the eastern frontier of the empire, were extending their influence eastwards and their missionaries would be reaching China by 635.[2] In Armenia, Syria and down the length of the Nile valley from Alexandria to Axum their rivals, the Monophysites — the "One-Nature Christians" — prevailed. These four great traditions have survived to our own day, supplemented by the insights of the Reformation and its daughter Churches.

How did this situation arise? Why should there ever have been "saints" and "sinners" in the New Covenant whose Founder and immediate followers envisaged as one body of the faithful? Was that ever a possible ideal, and do not the assertions of community of faith and practice that feature so strongly in the Pastoral Epistles (say c. 70-85) cover divisions that had existed in the Christian community since its origin? If so, how did Jesus' teaching, so clear and uncompromising and yet so free from credal formulae and definitions become the subject of such debate before the first century was out? By then some of those who claimed to be His followers were already being denounced as "shipwrecked in their faith" (1 Tim 1:19-20) and "handed over to Satan so that they might learn not to blaspheme" (Titus 3:10-11). The "heretical man" if persistent in his "blasphemies" should be shunned.

Heresy and orthodoxy were never static concepts, and for

---

[2]For the Nestorian missionary expansion through central Asia to China, see A. Mingana, "The Early Spread of Christianity in Central Asia and the Far East: a New Document," *Bulletin of the John Rylands Library* 9:2, 1925.

this reason alone I am not going to try to answer the
question put some 50 years ago by the great German scholar, Walter Bauer, in a work that has now been translated
under the title *Orthodoxy and Heresy in the Earliest Christianity*.[3] In the area where Christianity first established
itself, Palestine, western Asia Minor, around Antioch, in
Alexandria and in Rome, there were large Jewish communities whose members reacted differently to the preaching of
the disciples and Paul on the life, teaching and "mighty
works" (Acts 2:22) of Jesus. Even when that reaction was
positive and enthusiastic and Jesus was accepted as the
promised Messiah, those who became Christians themselves represented many varying tendencies within Judaism.
There is no point therefore in arguing whether "heresy" or
"orthodoxy" flourished first. Amid the fervent expectations
aroused by Paul's preaching, many contradictory ideas rose
to the surface, as is shown by the Christians addressed in 1
Corinthians. Some of these ideas would be accepted eventually as orthodox, others rejected as "false-teaching" and
"heresy." The emergence of conflicting views regarding the
teaching and organisation of the new Christian communities may well have been arising simultaneously wherever
Christianity took root. These divergencies were, moreover,
fueled by the fact that at the time of Christ, some of the
major Jewish communities, notably Antioch and Alexandria, were becoming associated with particular interpretations of Scripture, while in the background was the major
difference between Judaism of Jerusalem and Judaism of
the Dispersion. To all this, Christianity would be the explo-
sive heir.

Bauer's thesis has less relevance to our study than
expected, for the true origins of saints and sinners in the
early Church are to be found largely within Judaism itself.
Christians at the time of the Pastorals probably regarded
themselves as the bearers of the New Covenant with Israel,

---

[3] W. Bauer, *Orthodoxy and Heresy in Earliest Christianity* (trans. from 2nd ed.
by R. A. Kraft) (London, 1972), p. 29, for instance, regarding Edessa, and pp.
48-53, on Egypt.

prophesied by Jeremiah (31:31ff). This justified Paul's and their claims to be the "saints" ("chosen individuals" as in 2 Cor 13:15 and Jude 3), as described in Nehemiah (8:17) and Daniel (7:18) and as the Remnant, preserved as a "royal priesthood" and a new chosen people (1 Pet 2:9 = Exod 19:5-6) for God's service at a time when the rest of the Jewish people had failed. "I am the true vine" (Jn 15:1) was John's record of Jesus' claim, and the vine was the symbol of a living Judaism on the copper coins issued by the revolutionaries against Rome in the great uprising of 66-73.[4] In these conditions, it is entirely understandable that among the later books of the New Testament, the circular letters 1 Peter and James are both addressed to the tribes of the Jewish Dispersion. The Christians had fulfilled and upheld the Law through their faith (cf. Rom 2:31), and as Paul told the Galatians in c. 53 A.D. "If you are Christ's you are also Abraham's offspring" (Gal 3:29).

The relationship between Judaism and Christianity was therefore close and abiding. Christians would be reacting to teaching that was not acceptable to their leaders in much the same way as Jews would react. Judaism itself, however, throughout the first century was an extraordinarily complex and creative movement whose supreme achievements, it may be claimed, were summed up in the life and teaching of Jesus Christ and the career of Paul. Because of its vigour and creativity, it was far from being the monolithic movement that it appeared to be to outsiders. Monotheism, observance of the Law, its covenants and the hope that God would indeed save his people, formed a common bond between all who called themselves Jews. Jerusalem was the centre on which were focused the aspirations of all Jews, whether they lived in Palestine or in some Greek-speaking centre hundreds of miles away, and for each male Jew to send an annual contribution to the Temple treasury at Jerusalem was regarded as a privilege to be defended rather

[4]Illustrated in F. Madden, *History of Jewish Coinage* (London, 1864), p. 177, and in Y. Yadin, *Masada* (Leiden, 1971), p. 98.

than a grievance.[5] In addition, Judaism was a faith and way of life which demanded, and willingly received, sacrifices. While a wide variety of views prevailed among Jews as to the attitude they should adopt towards secular, pagan authorities, there was no doubt when their religion appeared to be threatened. Philo of Alexandria (c. 20 B.C. - c. 50 A.D.) and his younger contemporary, the historian Josephus (c. 37 -100 A.D.) were both men of the world who accepted the Roman Empire, Philo by conviction and Josephus largely through his experiences in the Jewish revolt. Both, however, were committed intensely to the Jewish religion and were prepared to accept the consequences of their faith. "A glorious death met in the defence of the Law is a new kind of life," Philo claimed, when the emperor Caligula (37-41) appeared to be planning to desecrate the Temple at Jerusalem.[6] Josephus, commenting on the supposed courage of the Jews, stated "one ought not to wonder at us if we are more courageous in dying than other men are," because "it becomes natural for all Jews immediately after birth to esteem those books (of the Law) above all to contain divine concepts, and to persist in them and if necessary to die for them."[7] Christian martyrdom was preceded by Jewish martyrdom.

Within this community, spread from one end of the Mediterranean to the other,[8] there were, however, divergences, tensions and potential conflicts. These affected matters even of belief such as the dispute over the resurrection between the Pharisees and the Sadducees (cf. Acts 23:7-9), as well as

[5]Thus Cicero, *Pro Flacco* 67, (Jews forbidden by the governor to send contributions to Jerusalem) and compare Josephus, *Antiquities* xvi 161, 171-172 (Jews permitted to send contributions to Jerusalem by decree). For Jerusalem as the capital of the Jewish world, see Philo, *Legatio* 36:281, ed. E. M. Smallwood (Leiden, 1961).

[6]Philo, *Legatio ad Gaium*, 29:192.

[7]Josephus, *Contra Apionem* 1:8.42, ed. H. St. J. Thackeray, and compare Philo, *op. cit.* 31:208 and 210.

[8]On the extent of the Dispersion, see the contemporary witness of Philo, *op. cit.* 36:281, and *In Flaccum* 43 and 46. For its prevalence in Asia Minor and Greece, see *Acts of the Apostles* 13-19 and in general, E. Schürer, *A History of the Jewish People* (Eng. trans. 1882), ii:3, pp. 220ff.

questions relating to authority and attitudes towards secular powers, especially the Roman Empire. Let us take two instances, priesthood and prophecy, and the ideal of the "gathered" against the "universal" community, both of which continue in the history of early Christianity. It does not require more than a casual reading of the Old Testament, particularly Kings and Samuel, to become aware of the tension between the priestly and prophetic in Israel. The priests served the temple of the Lord in an orderly urbanised environment. The prophets, such as Elijah, Elisha and Amos, were from the countryside (see 1 Kings 19:19 on Elisha), out of sympathy with the royal court and used to moving from place to place, accepting hardship, even living in caves (1 Kings 19:9), but in tune with "grass roots" Israelite opinions, and constantly issuing dire warnings about the penalties for backsliding from the worship of the Lord and denouncing the crimes of the rich. Later, as the moment of the crisis in Israel's fortunes drew near in 587 B.C., with Jerusalem itself threatened with capture, Jeremiah contrasted his role as a prophet with that of the unfortunate *Jehoiakim*, king of Israel. Announcing the Lord's command to him to prophesy, he said "And I, behold, I will make you this day a fortified city, an iron pillar, and bronze walls, against the whole land, against the kings of Judah, its princes and the people of the land" (Jer 1:18). It was a sense of integrity coupled with fearsome individualism, long to be remembered, and which would leave its traces on titles such as "pillar" and "wall" that were to be applied to the first generation of the Christian leadership. Peter, James and John were "pillars" (Gal 2:9) and James, the Lord's brother, was "the Wall" (Eusebius *H.E.* ii 23:7).[9] For these prophets of Old Israel, the wilderness and the heroic age of Israel rather than the Temple were to be the source of inspiration. In New Testament times, romantics depicted them as wandering about in "sheepskins and goatskins," persecuted by those who thought they knew better (Heb 11:37-38). John the Baptist and the Christian pro-

[9]Eusebius, *Historia Ecclesiastica* (= *H.E.*), ed. and trans. Kirsopp Lake, ii:23.7.

phetic movement of the Montanists in Phrygia and North Africa in the second and third centuries as well as the Covenanters of Q'mran were their heirs.

The prophets stood for no compromise with the outside, pagan world. Their ideal however could not be fulfilled. It was not simply that intermarriage with neighbouring tribes which the writer of Deuteronomy so feared (Deut 7:3-4) could not be avoided, but the development of Jerusalem as a trading centre involved increasing and fruitful contact with Gentiles. This brings us to the second example. Gradually, more outward-looking attitudes developed and in the years that followed the Babylonian Captivity (586-536 B.C.) these found a spokesman in the writer known to us as Second Isaiah. Instead of destroying the Gentiles and their gods, God's chosen people should act as their guides and examples, "to be a light to the Gentiles" (Isa 49:6; cf. 55:4). Proselytes from other nations were welcome, so that the house of Jahweh "shall be called a house of prayer for all peoples" (Isa 56:7).

The universal tendency in Judaism was to have a long history. Five centuries later, Philo opened his plea to the emperor Caligula with a description of the Jews "as the people who saw God," "the race of suppliants" for the rest of humanity.[10] Philo himself was no friend of Gentiles, least of all Greek settlers in Palestine,[11] but he believed that the best prospects for his people lay in accepting the protection of the Roman Empire, and his praise of Augustus as the ruler who brought peace to mankind was to be echoed in almost the same terms by the Christian Alexandrians, Origen and Eusebius.[12] A universal Jewish faith in a universal Roman Empire — such would seem to have been Philo's hope. It was, however, a hope to be frustrated by the narrow nationalist and ritualistic character of Judaism and its priestly leadership in Jerusalem. It could only come about when the national mould of Judaism was broken by Christianity at the Apostolic Council of 48.

[10] *Leg. ad Gaium*, 1:4.

[11] *Ibid.*, 30:200: criticism of Greek settlers in Jamnia.

[12] *Ibid.*, 21:144, and compare Origen, *Contra Celsum* ii:30.

This particularistic current, however, turned out to be the more acceptable to the Jewish people as a whole. We see it represented in Deuteronomy, in the prophet Ezekiel, and after the restoration of Jerusalem and the Temple by permission of the Persians c. 450 B.C. in the writings of Ezra, the scribe. In the small temple-state focused on Jerusalem during the fifth and fourth centuries B.C., the Jewish leaders emphasised the duty of all Jews scrupulously to follow out the prescriptions of the Law. Theirs was the cult of the "gathered community" — again, an expression we shall encounter in Christianity — the opposite to the missionary and comprehensive ideal of Second Isaiah. Jahweh reverted to his role as a warlike tribal god, jealous of his authority. His people became obsessed with their racial and religious purity and opposed vehemently to any association with outsiders.

The second factor one may mention briefly was emerging in this classic period of Israel's history. The relative dualism that had existed from an early period, through the theology of the Two Ways (Deut 30:15ff.) and the dichotomy between the Chosen People and the "nations" that formed one of the bridges between Judaism and early Christianity, became more pronounced through contact with Iranian Zoroastrianism. The fall of Jerusalem in 586 B.C. ushered in a long period of close and not unfruitful relationship between Israel and the great kingdoms, first Babylonian and then Persian, that dominated the Euphrates valley and further east. Not every Jew "sat down by the rivers of Babylon and wept" (Ps 137:1) and Babylon was to become the largest centre of Jewish religious and intellectual life after Jerusalem. Under the influence of the predominant dualistic religion of the Persian Empire, conflict between Jahweh and his enemies moved on to a cosmological plane. The heathen gods of Israel's enemies became forces of evil, eternal enemies of God and man. Speculation develops concerning the role of angels and demons. Satan became Anti-Christ. The Day of the Lord that saw the vindication of Israel and punishment of the nations, becomes heightened into apocalyptic visions of a millennium for the saved but for the mass of mankind fire and brimstone, that played so much part in the religious imagery of Judaism in the last centuries before Christ and in early Christianity.[13] Moreover, from speculation concerning the end of the world followed others concerning the relation of the imperfect world and its creator to the God of the universe. Could God be the author of evil as well as of good?

There would have been scope enough for the emergence of conflicting ideals within Judaism if Persian domination had continued indefinitely. As is well-known, the Persian Empire fell before the crushing defeats inflicted on it by Alexander the Great 334-331 B.C. The whole of the eastern Mediterranean was opened up to travel, commerce and the spread of ideas under the dominance of its new Macedonian masters. This was another turning point in the fortunes of Israel, for the Jews took their opportunity to move in considerable numbers out of Palestine and trade and settle in the empire of Alexander and his successors. The Jewish Dispersion in the Mediterranean area had come into being.

Through the third century B.C., the Jews were not unwelcome as traders and colonists. Instead, they were settled in large numbers by the Seleucid king Antiochus III in Phrygia and Lydia in Asia Minor as guardians of his interests against revolts by barbarous and unassimilated tribes.[14] During the next two centuries, Jews established themselves in almost every town of any size in the eastern Mediterranean, as far west as Carthage and in southeastern Spain, and in the trading towns along the North African coast.[15] The most important communities, however, were in western Asia Minor, in and around Antioch, in Cyrenaica, and above all in Alexandria. There, in the intellectual centre of the Mediterranean world, the Jews dominated two of the five quarters into which the city was divided and were represented in the others.[16] But it was Judaism with a differ-

[13]See the interesting article by C. N. Sneddon, "Zoroastrianism and Its Influence," *Modern Churchman* 31 (1941-1942), 507-515, and W. Bousset, *Antichrist* (Gottingen, 1895).

[14]Josephus, *Antiquities* xii: 150.

[15]See, for instance, P. Monceaux, *Histoire littéraire de l'Afrique chrétienne*, i (Paris, 1901) for North Africa.

[16]See E. M. Smallwood, ed., *Legatio*, pp. 5ff.

ence. The language of the Dispersion was Greek. While looking to Jerusalem as their centre — a sort of Mecca in the Jewish world — and perhaps going on pilgrimage there for one of the great festivals, their general way of life was Greek, with the all-important exception of religion.

The translation in Alexandria of the Hebrew Scriptures into Greek — the Septuagint — during the latter part of the third century B.C., provided Judaism in the Dispersion with a sacred literature for itself and a means of attracting converts. In the first century A.D., Acts 13-17 gives us a very good idea what a Jewish community in the Dispersion looked like. It was what we should call today a vigorous sub-culture. The core of Jews encountered by Paul on his missionary journey remained completely committed to their faith, but they were surrounded by a wide circle of those who attended synagogue worship but accepted only parts of the Mosaic law and remained Gentiles. These included, however, influential citizens in their communities, such as the "devout women of high standing" in Antioch of Pisidia (Acts 13:50), and it was educated people such as these who "searched the Scriptures diligently" (Acts 17:11) who were among those most influenced by Paul's preaching. Synagogues, as we know from the American excavations at Sardes, could be large and prominently-placed buildings.[17] In many ways, however, their adherents tended to turn their backs on their fellow townsmen. They had their own trade guilds, treasury, courts of justice administering, as Paul records (2 Cor 11:24-25), severe sentences, and they were buried in their own cemeteries. The tell-tale *Enthadé Keite* ("here lies") and the salutation *En Eiréné* ("in peace") are part of the Jewish legacy that has survived to our own day.[18]

Wealthy and vigorous though these Jewish communities were, Greek culture was all-pervading. It exercised an attraction that partially offset that of Judaism as a religion. Paul, whose education as a Pharisee had been more

[17]See A. T. Kraabel, "Paganism and Judaism: the Sardis Evidence," = pp. 13-33 of A. Benoit (ed.) *et al, Paganisme, Judaisme, Christianisme* (Paris, 1978).

[18]See E. Dinkler, "Eirene, der Urchristliche Friedengesdanke." *S. B. Heidelberger Acad. der Wissenschaften* 1973:1, pp. 7-47.

Jerusalem-oriented than that of most of his contemporaries, could not avoid some knowledge of Greek poets even if only from anthologies. The process of assimilation was continuous and nowhere more than in Alexandria. Here, Philo is the commanding figure, statesman, counsellor, and above all, philosopher. If Paul is the founder of a Christian theology, Philo was founder of a Christian philosophy.[19] Briefly, he attempted as a Jew to interpret Judaism and its Scriptures to his fellow-Jews in terms of Platonism. Jahweh was conceived as God of the universe. His Word, the Divine Logos was equated with Plato's *demiourgos* (craftsman), the agent of creation, and implicitly a second deity. The Scriptures were interpreted allegorically, i.e. that behind each verse, or word even, of the text lay a deeper, spiritual meaning discoverable by mental wrestling and contemplations and concepts drawn from Platonic philosophy. Thus Adam was equated with Mind created "after the image of God,"[20] and his and Eve's expulsion from Eden, the expulsion of evil-mindedness from the holy boundaries.[21] Eve represented the lesser quality of sense-perception,[22] but the personalities of Hagar and Sarah were interpreted as representing secular learning and higher wisdom respectively.[23] Paul was less complimentary, reducing Hagar to representation of the bondage of the Law, while Sarah stood for Jerusalem and freedom after the Spirit (Gal 4:24). Two centuries later, Clement of Alexandria was to borrow copiously from Philo.[24] His Divine Word had become personal-

[19]See H. Chadwick, "Philo," = ch. 8 of A. H. Armstrong, ed., *The Cambridge History of Later Greek and Early Mediaeval Philosophy* (Cambridge, 1967), p. 137.

[20]Philo, *Quis Her.* 231; for other references, see the list given in F. H. Colson and J. W. Earp, eds., *Philo X* (Loeb Library), p. 281.

[21]Philo, *Congr.* 171.

[22]Philo, *Leg. All* ii:5ff, 9, 14, 24, etc. (see also Colson and Earp, *op. cit.*, 311-315).

[23]*Leg. All.* iii:244 and *Soc.* 43ff., contrasting with Sarah, *Leg. All.* iii:244. Contrast Paul's interpretation, Sarah and Hagar representing the two covenants (Gal 4:24).

[24]See H. Chadwick, *Early Christian Thought and the Classical Tradition* (Oxford, 1966), pp. 55-57.

ised in Jesus Christ, "exact image of the Father."(c.f. Heb. 1:3) Already, even before the Crucifixion, some of the lines of future Alexandrian theology were being laid down.

All this time, the experience of Palestinian Jewry had been radically different. There, too, Greek influence had been penetrating throughout the third century B.C., but it had aroused much more resistance. The anti-heathen and anti-foreign tendencies in Palestinian Judaism never died out. The extension of the Seleucid realm to Palestine after Antiochus III's victory over the Ptolemies at the battle of Panium (Banias) in 198 B.C. at first led to an explicit guarantee of freedom for Jewish traditions. "All Jews may enjoy their traditional way of life,"[25] Antiochus declared. Under Antiochus III's successor but one, the able but vainglorious Antiochus IV (175-164 B.C.), a crisis developed. By this time many leading families in Jerusalem were welcoming Hellenisation; a gymnasium was built, the Greek ephebate instituted and even circumcision was in decline.[26]

Then Antiochus overreached himself. Partly to gain control of the Temple treasury and partly in an attempt to unify his empire, "he wrote," said the writer of the official history of the Hasmonean dynasty, "that all should be one people" (1 Macc 1:4). Unfortunately that involved the assimilation of Jahweh and the Temple-state of Jerusalem to the level of other local Baals and their territories and ultimately the erection of Antiochus' statue in the Temple court and the sacrifice of swine (1 Macc 1:45). In addition, in order to draw the teeth of a xenophobic Torah, Sabbath observance and circumcision were forbidden. "It was unlawful for a man to profess himself a Jew." So wrote the author of 2 Maccabees (2 Macc 6:1-8).

Antiochus underestimated the likely strength of opposition. The pattern of events often to be repeated in Jewish and early Christian history unfolded during 167 and the following years. There was a civil war.[27] Some, mainly in the

[25]Josephus, *Antiquities*, xii:142 — together with a tax exemption for three years.

[26]1 Maccabees 1:11-14; compare 2 Macc 4:12-14.

[27]Josephus, *Ant.* xiii:1 ("Godless" Jewish supporters of Bacchides).

towns, accepted the king's orders. Others, particularly in the countryside around Jerusalem, went into open revolt. This was the first recorded genuine example of a war of religion, and in the end the rebels won. In 142 B.C. the Seleucids finally abandoned their attempts to govern Jerusalem and Simon Maccabaeus, the eldest surviving member of the Hasmonaean clan that had first raised the standard of revolt, was declared by the people "their governor and chief priest" (1 Macc 14:25). The conflict had resulted in great losses among the Jews, but also the beginning of a tradition of martyrs and martyrdom,[28] and associated with that, belief in the resurrection of fallen heroes (Dan 12:2) and then, by extension, of all true Israelites (cf. Jn 11:24). It also led to the emergence of groups, whom Josephus describes as "parties" (*haireseis*)[29] among whom were the forerunners of the Pharisees who were devoted to understanding and achieving an ever more exact interpretation of the Law. Above all, it engendered a lasting hostility between the Palestinian Jews and their non-Jewish neighbours. Jerusalem, the Temple, and its worship were from now on the centre of a self-conscious cult and a thoroughly xenophobic state. Its people regarded as enemies not only pagans in the surrounding territories but the kindred Samaritans who were dismissed as half-castes and misbelievers to be shunned by the true Jews.[30] It is difficult not to find in Palestinian Jewish attitudes towards religious unorthodoxy one root of the harshness exercised by the early Christians against those who deviated from the prevalent tradition of orthodoxy.

One must not contrast, however, too heavily the differences between Judaism in Palestine and the Dispersion. In Palestine itself, Greek remained the second language and as the story of Simon of Cyrene shows (Mk 15:21) there were

[28]See the present author's *Martyrdom and Persecution in Early Christianity* (Oxford, 1965), pp. 49ff.

[29]Josephus, *Antiquities*, xiii:171.

[30]Josephus, *Ant.*, xiii:280 (ruthless destruction of Samaria by John Hyrcanus). Compare New Testament times, John 4:9 (Jews have no dealings with the Samaritans) and for the Samaritans' attitude to the Jews, Luke 9:52-53.

plenty of comings and goings between Jews from the Dispersion and the homeland. In Asia Minor, Acts 19:1 indicates the presence at Ephesus of a community committed to John the Baptist's teaching, while at Teuchira (Tokra) in Cyrenaica the Jewish cemetery contained no less than one quarter of some 400 graves belonging to individuals who retained close links with the Jewish homeland.[31] Moreover, 2 Maccabees showed that the Dispersion produced Jews no less anti-Greek and anti-pagan as were Palestinian Jews. Nonetheless, differences of language, the absence of the Temple and its cult, and the pressures towards assimilation resulted in divergencies of outlook, which may be reflected in the teaching and attitudes of Jesus and Paul respectively.

For Palestine in Jesus' time, to the world of "scribes, Pharisees, hypocrites," so one-sidedly described in the Gospels, one must add the all-important element of the Essenes and Covenanters of the Dead Sea. The Essenes, like the Pharisees, are described as a "Hairesis" by Josephus,[32] and the advanced social teaching that they expressed has now found confirmation from a completely unexpected quarter. The discovery of the Scrolls and the fact that the Covenanters were contemporaries with the ministry of Jesus and the emergence of the primitive Christian community have stirred New Testament studies as nothing since the Renaissance. The Scrolls help place Jesus in his Palestinian setting, for the Covenanters also expected the rapid end of the Age, they were concerned with membership of the Kingdom and they associated piety and poverty with its requirements. If they are to be associated with the Essenes, they also reject personal property, and in contrast to every movement of the day, whether within or without Judaism, they also rejected slavery.[33]

In contrast, however, to both Jesus and his community, the Covenanters believed in the forceful overthrow of idola-

---

[31]See S. Appelbaum, "The Jewish Community at Teuchira," *Scripta Hierosolymitana* 7 (1961), pp. 27-48 at pp. 40-48.

[32]*Antiquities*, iii:172.

[33]Philo, *Quod omnis probus homo liber sit*, ed. F. H. Colson, xii:76-80.

try powers of this world. The War Scroll (six copies of which have been found at Q'mran) with its minute instructions for the conduct of Armageddon, and the finding of fragments of Scroll-like documents at Masada suggest that they meant what they wrote.[34] Jews, whether in Palestine or the Dispersion, had this factor in common. They were a minority and they felt all the frustrations of a vigorous minority that believes in the ultimate righteousness of its cause against those whom they think of as oppressors.

Jewish attitudes, however, towards their pagan neighbours and the Roman imperial authorities ranged through an entire spectrum. Sicarii and Zealots on the one hand, relative loyalists such as the Sadducean high-priesthood and many of the Pharisees on the other, reflected a confusion of hopes and ideals.[35] Jesus' disciples were not unaffected by these attitudes. Some believed that Jesus "would restore the Kingdom of Israel" (Acts 1:6), and that kingdom was conceived as an independent state enjoying at least the boundaries of King David's realm. It was a kingdom in which, as had been shown during the eighty years of Jewish independence between the end of the Maccabean wars and Pompey's capture of Jerusalem in 63 B.C., Gentiles would have no part. For those who believed that the necessary political change would be brought about by the Messiah, the approach to his coming would be heralded by upheavals of every sort, persecutions, earthquakes, wars, famines and pestilence, such were the Messianic woes, symbolized for all time in popular imagination by the Four Horsemen of the Apocalypse (Rev 6:1-8).

Such were some elements in Judaism that made it so creative and purposeful a movement within the Greco-Roman world in the first century A.D. It combined insistence on right practice ("Covenant") as well as right worship, duty to one's neighbour as well as duty to God. Christianity,

[34] For the War Scroll, see M. Baillet, *Q'mran Grotte 4*, vol. iii (= *Discoveries in the Judean Desert* vii)(Oxford, 1982), ch. ii, and for the possibility of the Covenanters being at Masada, see Yadin, *Masada*, 172-175.

[35] See H. Loewe, *Render unto Caesar* (Cambridge, 1940), pp. 40ff., and for the Zealots, E. Schürer (eds. F. Millar and G. Vermes), *The History of the Jewish People in the Age of Jesus Christ*, vol. ii (London, 1979), pp. 599-606.

while insisting that Christ's Kingdom was not of this world, inherited most of these attitudes and problems, and could hardly be less creative than its predecessor and rival. Whatever the aspirations of the Gospel-writers and Paul and his successors towards unity, the Church could not avoid being a melting pot of diverse and even conflicting ideals. It could never be an idealised community as portrayed in Acts 4:32-36 nor a monolithic structure as indicated in Eph 4:5 (One Lord, one faith, one baptism). Baptism and acceptance of Jesus Christ as Lord and Messiah, and belief in his Coming with Judgement at the end of the Age formed the common bond between all who called themselves Christians, but otherwise they were as little united as the Jews who disowned them with such bitter emphasis.

One can already see some contrasting tendencies emerging in the Pauline communities. Paul's preaching took the Jewish communities in the Dispersion in western Asia Minor and Greece by storm. Between 47 and 57 A.D., he had literally turned the Jewish world upside down. He had told the Gentile semi-proselytes exactly what they wanted to hear. As he explained to the Galatians, in Jesus Christ they were all "sons of God through faith" (Gal 3:26-27). The Law had been of negative value only, "until faith should be revealed" (Gal 3:23) while at the same time the baneful power of the planetary deities ("the elemental spirits of the universe," Gal 4:4) had been overthrown. Mankind was now free. There was neither Jew nor Greek, slave or free, male or female; all were one in Christ Jesus. No wonder the Galatians received him as "an angel of God" (Gal 4:14) and the Thessalonians with like enthusiasm (Thess 1:6). His success, however, unleashed all the latent tensions within the Dispersion communities. It was like opening Pandora's box. "We are kings" (1 Cor 4:8) was the reaction of the Corinthians. The Law was no more. Everything was possible. Scholars who have traced the origins of Gnostic libertinism and dualism back to early interpretations of Paul's message have not been wholly mistaken.[36] It would fall to the next genera-

---

[36]Thus, Morton Smith, *Clement of Alexandria and a Secret Gospel of Mark* (Cambridge, Mass.: 1973), pp. 259-260.

tion of Christian leaders to try to sort out the problems resulting from the Pauline revolution.

Here I emphasise the role of Paul, for the first generation after the disappearance from the scene of Peter and Paul saw the Church decline in Jesus' homeland but advance in the Dispersion beyond the limits of the Pauline mission. The fall of Jerusalem in 70 was a catastrophe for the Church in Palestine as it was for Judaism. "Moderates" are seldom loved in times of crisis. Though social revolution against property owners in Palestine failed, the leadership of the Jewish people passed to the Pharisees. They ensured that the Christians would be excluded from the community of Israel. Within Judaism the pressures of a rival claimant to the allegiance of the Jewish people as well as pressures of war had resulted in the deadly equation of misbelief-blasphemy, for which the punishment was scourging,[37] or, if opportunity permitted, death.

For the Christians, however, the destruction of the Temple and the end of Jerusalem as the political and religious centre of Judaism involved a fresh source of division. James' church had represented tradition, priestly successsion from the apostles and ultimately from Christ, and a visible headship of the Christian *Ecclesia*.[38] That would now fade rapidly and with its decline went the decline also of the interpretation of Jesus' message in his own language, Aramaic. In the Dispersion, however, the churches Paul had founded weathered the storm. They began to flourish despite the pressures exercised by adherents of normative Judaism and judaisers. From the towns of Western Asia Minor, Christianity set out to conquer the Greco-Roman world. It was, however, a Greek Christianity with a synagogue-based organisation while Paul, believing that the Coming was at hand, had never fixed a centre of authority

[37]Thus, John 9:22, and Justin Martyr, *Dialogue with Trypho* 47:1, ed. and trans. A. Lukyn Williams. For the Jewish demand that the death penalty be inflicted on Paul, see Acts 24 and 25.

[38]See A. A. T. Ehrhardt, *The Apostolic Succession*, pp. 64ff. Hegesippus (flor. circa 175) "saw in St. James the true successor entering the Holy Place" (Eusebius, *H.E.*, ii:23.6).

nor established any institutions to judge whether particular beliefs were acceptable or not. Differing ideas of hierarchy were developing, including successions from prophets or even family successions.[39] It is only by inference that one may attribute some sort of leadership to Ephesus and to its ruler, John the presbyter, near the end of the century.

We may now return to the problem we started with. How far do the Pastorals reflect the real world of early Christianity? Unfortunately, the compilers tell us little about the actual beliefs the false teachers were spreading. The vehemence of their denunciations, however, indicates that in their minds misbelief was in some way connected with moral turpitude. Heretics were to be rebuked and avoided. Debate was useless (2 Tim 2:14, 16, 23). From about 50 A.D. onwards a point of transition had been approached in both Judaism and Christianity whereby "hairesis" became "heresy" and took on the negative meaning it was to retain henceforth.[40] When Paul wrote to the Corinthians in c. 53 (1 Cor 11:19) that "sects and heresies were necessary so that the truth might be manifest," he seems to have had in mind the necessity of maintaining the unity of the new People by rejecting the blandishments of divisive judaising opponents, and perhaps those who drew unacceptable implications (libertine!) from his preaching of freedom in Christ. In Galatians (5:20) he includes "heresies" with "strife and sedition" and in general with the "works of the flesh." However, in 58 A.D., Paul could defend the "heresy" of the Pharisees in believing in the resurrection of the dead (Acts 24:14).

Perhaps under the challenge of Christianity, Judaism was moving along parallel lines. In the same year, 58, Tertullus, the lawyer hired by the Jews in Jerusalem, accused Paul of being the ringleader of a pestilential sect (*hairesis*) bent on

---

[39]For the idea of an Apostolic succession of Christian prophets in parts of Asia Minor, see Ehrhardt, *op. cit.*, p. 69, and for episcopal succession being kept in one family, see the case of Polycrates (second-century Ephesus), quoted in Eusebius (*H.E.*, vi:24.4).

[40]See A. Momigliano, 'Empieta ed Eresia nel Mondo Antico," *Rivista Storica Italiana* 83:4 (1971), 282, and M. Simon, "From Greek Hairesis to Christian Heresy" in *Early Christian Literature and the Classical Intellectual Tradition, Festschrift Robert Grant*, ed. W. Schoedel (Paris, 1979), pp. 101-116.

subverting the teaching of Moses (Acts 24:1-6).

At this stage, conflict was focussed on the borderlands of Church and Synagogue. The culprits in the Pastorals seem to be almost entirely Jews or Judaisers, "men of the circumcision" (Titus 1:10), who "quarreled over the law" (3:9), but were also active missionaries "subverting whole families" (1:11). In detail, these people were interested in genealogies and associated "myths." They were ascetically-minded, requiring abstinence from certain foods and forbidding marriage (1 Tim 4:3). They were thus demonstrating negative attitudes towards the basic institutions of the created world and by implication its Creator. Perhaps, as the Norwegian scholar, Oscar Skarsaune, has suggested, this would correspond to a purely spiritual conception of the resurrection of the body.[41] Their claim that "the resurrection was past already" (2 Tim 2:18) meant that they had already died to the world and risen again with Christ at their baptism. (Compare Rom 6:3ff. and Col 2:12 for justification of this idea in Paul.) Finally, they were maintaining that knowledge (*gnosis*) was more important than adherence to any accepted tradition of belief (1 Tim 6:20). Judaising and seditious innovations had become the enemies of "tradition."

Judaism was also having to contend with those who denied the unity of God, the goodness of the Creator's handiwork and the election of Israel. These were the *minim*, and like their Christian counterparts they associated moral depravity with misbelief.[42] The development of the rival religions remained close. One sees it in the passage in 1 Timothy where the compiler mentions the names of the two Egyptian magicians, Iannes and Iambres, said to have defied Moses (2 Tim 3:8). The Exodus story of the incident (Exod 7:11) gives no names, but they appear in the Essene

[41]O. Skarsaune, "2 Timothy 2:18 and the Concept of Heresy in Apostolic and Post-Apostolic Times," unpublished lecture delivered at Oslo University, 7 May 1982. Also, G. W. H. Lampe, "Grievous Wolves," in *Christ and Spirit in the New Testament* (Cambridge, 1973), ed. B. Lindars and S. S. Smalley.

[42]Thus, M. Simon, *From Greek Hairesis*, p. 106 (= p. 826 of his *Collected Works*).

(?) *Damascus Document* and also in the Targum of Pseudo-Jonathan.[43]

The close-knit yet supra-national character of the early Christian communities favoured a strict interpretation of the New Covenant they, like the Essenes,[44] claimed to represent. They were the "royal priesthood," the bearers of the Spirit in the short *interim* period that would precede the Coming. It was now that false prophets preaching false beliefs could be expected, and these must be exposed and denounced. Within the framework, however, of acceptable beliefs and organisation in the Christian community, a wide variety of opinions and structures were existing to become the source of future conflicts. One obvious example was the attitude of Christians towards the empire. In view of what we have said already, it is not surprising that we find Christian attitudes similar to those in Judaism. Jesus' teaching and his example of submission to Pontius Pilate indicated the acceptability of a loyal attitude towards the empire and its authorities. The military Davidic messiahship had been rejected (Mk 8:31). Paul found no difficulty in following the loyalist tradition of some Pharisees, such as ben Zakhai and Josephus. "The powers that be are of God" and were to be obeyed (Rom 13:1-6). Similar advice was given emphatically in the Pastorals (1 Tim 2:2) and 1 Peter (1 Peter 2:17). Pauline Christianity, revolutionary by implication so far as the protecting deities of the empire were concerned, was not subversive to the institutions of the empire, including slavery.[45] Paul's appeal had been to educated and propertied hearers, not the inhabitants of the "highways and byways" of the eastern Mediterranean.

Side by side with this loyalist tradition, however, was another, more strident and aggressive, associated with prophets and martyrs in the Church. The contrast between

---

[43] *Damascus Document* 7:19—8:2, ed. R. H. Charles. Compare Menachoth 85a, and *Encyclopedia Biblica* 2357. I owe this information to Dr. Skarsaune.

[44] *Damascus Document* 8.

[45] See the discussion of G. E. M. de Ste. Croix, "Early Christian Attitudes towards Property and Slavery," *Studies in Church History* xii, ed. L. R. D. Baker (Oxford, 1974), pp. 1-38.

the Pastorals and *Revelation* is enormous. Rome is "the great whore of Babylon," "drunk with the blood of the saints" (Rev 17:5-6), and the martyrs themselves "crying out for vengeance" (6:10), whose prayers would be answered in a Coming and Judgement accompanied by a panorama of destruction and catastrophe. Revelation does not stand alone. In the early years of the second century, the prophet Hermas also visited on his readers the vision of the "great tribulation," derived perhaps from the Jewish III *Sibyllines* that foresaw persecution and suffering as the lot of the Christian before deliverance.[46] Not surprisingly, prelacy and prophecy were beginning to emerge as issues in the Church. The problem of the role and status of the residential Christian leader, the presbyter or bishop, could be seen to conflict with that of the itinerant prophet and teacher, particularly when the latter's message was one of doom.

The Coming, however, was delayed. What then of Christian worship and the personality of the Founder; how was Christ to be worshipped "as a god"?[47] And the nature of the Church and its mission: was it to be a "gathered community," a sect directed by prophets and other men and women of the Spirit awaiting the signs of the End, or was it to be in the world, possessed of a leadership able to adapt to the needs of a universal mission? How would the tradition "once for all delivered to the saints" (Jude 3) be interpreted and enforced among widely scattered communities in the Mediterranean? The Heretics, too, were confronting their opponents with the need of formulating credible answers to their questions. He who called into question the validity of the Law of Moses could find himself degrading the role of the Creator whose will Moses had interpreted. Questions that could not be answered from the teaching of the Gospels alone were beginning to crowd in. By the end of the first century the Church was finding itself the heir to existing conflicts within Judaism and to additional controversies

[46] III *Sibyllines*, lines 32ff., ed. and trans. H. N. Bate (London, 1918), "pestilence afflicting all mankind, who are brought low under the terror of judgment." For Hermas' vision of persecution and judgment, see *Vis.* iii:2.1.

[47] Pliny, *Ep.* x:96.7.

arising from its claim to be Israel. Saints and sinners were beginning to emerge according to their interpretation of the New Covenant, and perhaps also according to the location of the community to which they belonged.

Source Material

Bauer, W. *Orthodoxy and Heresy in Earliest Christianity*, ed. R. A. Kraft and G. Krodel. Philadelphia, 1971.

Bornkamm, G., *Jesus of Nazareth*. New York, 1975.

Black, Matthew, *The Essene Problem*. London, 1961.

Cross, F. M., *The Ancient Library of Qumran and Modern Biblical Studies*. Garden City, N.Y., 1958.

Daniélou, Jean, *The Theology of Jewish Christianity*. Philadelphia, 1977.

Davies, W. D., *Paul and Rabbinic Judaism*. London, 1980.

Grant, Michael, *Saint Paul*. New York, 1976.

Hengel, M., *Judaism and Hellenism*, 2 vols. Philadelphia, 1975.

Knox, W. L., *St. Paul and the Church of the Gentiles*. Cambridge, 1939.

Meeks, W., *The First Urban Christians*. New Haven, Conn., 1983.

Roberts, C. H., *Manuscript, Society and Belief in Early Christian Egypt*. London, 1979.

Schürer, Emil, *The History of the Jewish People in the Age of Jesus Christ*, ed. F. Millar and G. Vermes, 2 vols. Edinburgh, 1973 and 1979.

Simon, M., *Verus Israel*, 2nd ed. Paris, 1964.

Telfer, W., *The Office of a Bishop*. London, 1962.

Wolfson, H. A., *Philo*, 2 vols. Cambridge, 1947.

2

Plato or Scripture: The Choice Before the Gentile Church

We left the Church at the beginning of the second century in a far from coherent state. However powerful the ideal of unity in belief and organisation might be, circumstances were proving too strong. One of the legacies of Paul's tremendous successes in preaching the Gospel among the Dispersion communities had been to transfer many of the debates within Judaism to its Christian rival, where they were to have far-reaching effects on the life and teaching of the early Church.

Down to the failure of the Jewish revolt of 132-135, Christianity continued to exist to a great extent within the thought-world of Judaism. A visitor to Ephesus, for instance, during that period might have had some difficulty in differentiating between the orthodox Jewish and Christian communities in the town. John the presbyter, the leader of the latter, wore the insignia (the *petalon*) of a Jewish high-priest on his brow, and clearly considered himself the leader of the Jewish community there.[1] He was followed by a clan of bishops who through eight successive tenures kept

[1] Polycrates, *ap.* Eusebius, *H.E.* v:24, just as Epiphanius, *Panarion* 30, 38:4-5, writes of James of Jerusalem.

the office within their family, such as should be expected of a rabbinical or priestly succession in Judaism.[2] When both Jews and Christians reproached each other with being "hypocrites" on questions of timing their prayers and fasts,[3] but otherwise seemed to represent similar outlooks towards their Gentile neighbours, our visitor might be pardoned his confusion. Among the Christian communities themselves he would have found some bewildering differences. If he had visited the church led by Ignatius of Antioch, he would have experienced a theory and practice of episcopal leadership which elevated the bishop to something approaching the monarchical status of James of Jerusalem and his Jewish high-priestly counterpart.[4] This status, he would have found out, was not based on tradition but on claims of a more mystical nature that associated the bishop directly with Jesus Christ, the heavenly high-priest,[5] as set forth in an anonymous letter addressed to "the Hebrews."[6] In Asia Minor, on the other hand, leadership in each community was tending to fall into the hands of a single bishop, who represented tradition in teaching and practice that was alleged to go back to the words of the Apostles and to Jesus Christ himself. A stay at the church of Polycarp, Bishop of Smyrna, would have convinced him of the reality of episcopal government[7] in a major Christian community. He would be left wondering, however, what had happened to the "apostles and prophets" on whom Paul had declared (Eph 2:20) that the household of God was founded, Jesus Christ

[2] Eusebius, *H.E.* v:24.6.

[3] *Didache* 8:1.

[4] Ignatius was clearly aware of the high status he was claiming for himself, for in *Ep. ad Rom.* 4:3, he puts himself on a level at least to be compared with that of Peter and Paul. See W. Telfer, *The Office of Bishop*, (London, 1962), pp. 71-73.

[5] Ignatius, *Smyrn.* 8, where Ignatius makes the bishop the representative of Christ, while the presbyters represent the Apostles. Compare also *Trall.* 2.

[6] Not quoted, however, directly by Ignatius.

[7] See H. von Campenhausen, *Ecclesiastical Authority and Spiritual Power*, Eng. tr. J. A. Baker (London, 1969), pp. 157ff., though his dating of the Pastoral Epistles to "about the middle of the second century" seems to me to be far too late.

himself being the cornerstone. He would have to be aware of a teaching manual known as the "Teaching of the Twelve Apostles" (The *Didachē*) to discover that bishops were supposed to be "meek men" (*Did* 15:1) and that authority to teach and celebrate the Eucharist still lay with the proven authentic prophet.

The actual teaching of the various groups within each community would not have clarified the picture. While something approaching monarchical bishops were beginning to emerge in communities as far apart as Rome, Smyrna and Antioch, even within this framework of incipient orthodoxy varieties of belief persisted.[8] At Rome, Clement, the church's representative writing to the church at Corinth whose people were at odds with each other, indicates belief in a Trinity of Father, Son and Holy Spirit,[9] but seems to be using a version of New Testament Scripture which did not find its way into the canon.[10] At Antioch, Ignatius seems to have been constantly in dispute with people who claimed to be Christians, yet insisted on observing Jewish customs and maintained that Jesus' ministry was not a real ministry.[11] They may have imagined it as some prolonged angelic visitation such as that by angels who appeared to Abraham under the oak of Mamre. The Docetic Christology that this involved was raising moral as well as philosophical problems. "Would one die for a phantom?", Ignatius asked indignantly.[12] Even in Polycarp's community, where normative Christianity based on tradition was emerging most strongly, a negative view of God as Creator as reflected in Jewish (Old Testament) Scripture was being preached by a young man from Sinope named Marcion.[13] These situations were forcing even the most

[8]See my *The Early Church* (Philadelphia, 1981), p. 42, concerning Polycarp of Smyrna's church.

[9]*1 Clement* 42:3 and 58:2.

[10]Thus, a variant version of the Parable of the Sower, in *1 Clement* 24:5.

[11]Ignatius, *Philad.* 6, and compare, for Docetism, *Smyrn.* 5.

[12]Ignatius, *Smyrn.* 4.

[13]Polycarp, *Letter to Philippians* 7:1, and for Polycarp's reported encounter with Marcion, see Irenaeus, *Ad. Haer.* iii:3.4.

pragmatic leaders to think out some unexpected implications of the New Covenant.

Added to this, by circa 130 Christianity was at least beginning to penetrate the authentically Gentile world. Justin Martyr came from Neapolis (Nablus) in Samaria, born of a Greek settler parentage, and though the area was saturated with Samaritan and Jewish influences, he never considered conversion to Judaism. Instead, he tried out a round of current philosophical schools, found all unsatisfactory for his religious quest, and ultimately faced the alternatives of life as a Platonist or a Christian philosopher.[14] He chose the latter. His conversion, probably at Ephesus c. 135, was a sign of the times. Others were beginning to look beyond acceptance of ecclesiastical tradition or the fervid expectations of apocalyptic, towards a formulation of Christianity in terms of religious philosophy. At this very moment, in Alexandria, another Christian philosopher, Basilides, was attempting to construct a Christian way of salvation through a coalescence of elements of Judaism and Platonism focussed on Christ as Saviour, and not uninfluenced by current anti-Jewish feeling.[15] Apart from their common concern to present Christianity as a philosophy worthy of the support of educated contemporaries, Basilides and Justin went their separate ways. Justin became a pioneer of orthodox theology, a confessor and martyr. Basilides' theology formed part of what became known as the Gnostic movement. A century and a half later he was regarded as one of the founding fathers of an even more serious threat to orthodoxy, namely Manichaeism.[16] Meanwhile, first in Asia Minor and then in Rome, a third Christian thinker and leader, Marcion, was attempting to show that Christianity had no relation whatsoever to Judaism, but was God's free

[14]Justin, *Dialogue with Trypho* 2-7.

[15]For a sketch of Basilides' life and many extant quotations from his works preserved in Irenaeus and Clement of Alexandria, see W. Foerster, *Gnosis*, Eng. tr. R. McL. Wilson (Oxford, 1972), pp. 59-83, and also article by F. J. Hort in *Dictionary of Christian Biography* i, 268-281.

[16]Thus, Anonymous, *Acta Archelai* 55, ed. C. Beeson, *Die griechischen christlichen Schriftsteller der ersten drei Jahrhunderte* (= *GCS*) 16 (Leipzig, 1906).

gift through Christ. He "made all things new" (cf. Rev 21:5). His was "the new heaven and the new earth" promised to all who confessed to be Christians (Rev 21:1). This was the common appeal that was beginning to bring pagans into "the Great Church" or its rivals from c. 130 onwards.

We concentrate here on Basilides and Marcion. The *gnosis* that Basilides claimed to possess and to disseminate to his followers means "knowledge." At Alexandria he was the first of a brilliant trio of teachers who dominated the scene there between 130-180 and whose influence extended to Rome, Asia Minor and even among the Christians in the merchant communities from Asia Minor settled in the Rhone valley. Historically one can see them in the same line of descent as Philo, as those who sought to understand an essentially particularist monotheistic faith in terms of the most penetrating philosophic system of the day, namely Platonism.

Though their views were far from those of Philo and would have been combatted vigorously by him, they sought to arrive at the truth through the same process of intellectual insight and allegorical interpretation of Scripture as he had demonstrated a century before.[17]

Gnosticism has been among the most elusive problems of early Christianity. It is, however, one where archaeological discovery and research has achieved most towards their understanding and solution. The emergence of the Alexandrian school of teachers with Basilides, c. 130, had been preceded by two generations at least of teachers in Syria and Asia Minor. These, represented by Menander, Satornilus and Cerinthus, may perhaps illustrate early and perhaps instinctive endeavors to substitute the saving gospel of Jesus for what many Jews, including Paul, had come to regard as the insensitive teaching of the Law and its God, Jahweh. Thus, we find one of the Syrian Gnostics, Satornilus, c. 120, teaching that Jesus Christ came to undo the work and destroy the God of the Jews, and save all who believed in

---

[17]For Philo as a forerunner of Alexandrian Gnosticism, see R. McL. Wilson, *The Gnostic Problem* (London, 1958), ch. ii.

Him.[18] In his system of ideas, God and the creator of the material universe were utterly opposed beings.

Alexandria, however, provided Gnosticism with its most fertile ground, and Basilides, Valentinus and Heracleon have all left their mark on the history of Christianity. They deserved the reluctant respect of their opponents, such as Clement of Alexandria c. 200 A.D.,[19] for theirs was the originality of mind in an age when Christianity was very often associated with blind faith and anti-social prejudice.[20] They sought to widen the scope of Christianity from a personal search for the Kingdom through inner integrity that led to love towards God and one's neighbour to a philosophic religion that attempted to solve the ultimate moral and intellectual problems of existence, and of good and evil, that man has asked but never solved.

Their emergence was timely for, by 110-120, the approximate period when 2 Peter was written, the Second Coming was fading increasingly into the distance. Scepticism was rising (2 Peter 3:2) and even Paul's message was being critically discussed (ibid., 3:16). Some new impetus was needed. If the writer of the letter to the Hebrews had spoken of Christians as "enlightened" (Heb 6:5), and having tasted the gift of the Spirit, the Alexandrian Gnostics inquired what was "enlightenment"? How did one come to "know oneself" (a Stoic, not a Biblical, question), what was the object of existence, what was the origin of evil, what of man himself?[21] They believed that this understanding was attainable by what we should call intuitive knowledge (in the New Testament, perhaps the flash of insight that came to Paul on the road to Damascus) mediated by teachers who could claim the authority of Christ himself, and whose credentials

[18]Cited from Irenaeus, *Adv. Haer.* 1:24.2.

[19]Clement of Alexandria, *Stromata* vii:106, and compare Origen, *Comment. in Johannem* vi:23, ed. E. Preuschen, *GCS* 10 (1903) and vi:29 (praising exegesis by Heracleon).

[20]Celsus, quoted by Origen, *Contra Celsum*, Eng. trans. by H. Chadwick (Cambridge, 1953), 1:9.

[21]Some of the questions Tertullian (circa 200) says the Gnostics were asking, *De Praescriptione* 7.

were superior to three of the clergy of the "Great Church." It was not baptism by water that freed the Christians from the powers of Fate and the astral deities, but knowledge. "We alone," the Gnostics claimed, "know the unutterable mysteries of the spirit."[22] Only those who had been initiated into knowledge could bring order into the disorder of the visible world. They were "the true brothers" on whom the love of the Father had been poured.[23] The Bridal Chamber was for free men and virgins.[24]

The Gnostic outlook was therefore that of an elite, though one that embraced men and women as equals. Without ever stressing the Women's Lib element in their outlook, the anonymous Gnostic gospels, probably of second and early-third century, play up the role of Jesus' female companions and criticise the attitude of the disciples towards them.[25] Thus the *Gospel of Philip* says openly that Mary Magdalene was "loved by Jesus more than (he loved) the disciples," and that he used "to kiss her often on her mouth."[26] In the *Gospel of Mary* (Magdalene) the disciples, thoroughly disheartened after the Crucifixion, ask Mary to encourage them by telling them what the Lord had told her secretly. Her revelations, however, are badly received and Peter angrily asks, "Did he really speak privately with a woman, and not openly to us? Are we to turn about and all listen to her? Did he prefer her to us?" Mary asks whether he thought she was lying. Peter's indignation was going too far and Levi stepped in. "Peter, you have always been hot-tempered...If the Saviour made her worthy, who are you indeed to reject her?"[27] The tendency to bring out the personal weaknesses of the prince of the apostles emerges clearly in some Gnostic documents, and is combined here with criticism of the

[22]The Ophite (People of the Serpent) sect, circa 200, cited by Hippolytus, *Refutatio* v:8.26. Compare Irenaeus, *Adv. Haer.* 1:13.6.

[23] *The Gospel of Truth* 43, ed. J. Robinson, p. 49.

[24] *The Gospel of Philip* 69, ed. J. Robinson, p. 141.

[25]See, for the emphasis placed on the female aspects of Gnosticism, E. Pagel's *The Gnostic Gospels* (London, 1980), pp. 60-69.

[26] *Gospel of Philip* 63, ed. J. Robinson, p. 138.

[27] *Gospel of Mary* 17-18, ed. J. Robinson, p. 473.

self-sufficiency of "open tradition" in the Church.

Though men and women could equally share the illumination and secrets of Gnosticism, the numbers of the saved were few. They were known, it was claimed, "by God before they were begotten."[28] On the analogy of the Platonic division of the human being into body, mind and spirit, the Gnostics also divided humanity into three parts. There were first the spiritual beings (*pneumatikoi*), those illumined by Gnosis, whose souls were destined to return to their home with God. Then there was a larger group, the "people of the soul" (*psychikoi*), which in practice included orthodox Christians, who were capable of receiving illumination, and the great majority, slaves of matter, who were destined to death, destruction and oblivion.

The road to Knowledge was in practice not so free from earthly toil as some of the critics of Gnosticism would have us believe. While some sects, notably the Carpocratians, understood liberty from the Law as freedom from every sort of moral restraint in the destruction of the works of the Creator, most Gnostic writings stress the virtues of abstinence and asceticism. Study of the religious beliefs and associated ascetic practices of ancient people such as the Phrygians, Egyptians and Indians were cited as examples to follow.[29] They, too, had arrived at truths that the Gnostics claimed to possess. Old Testament Scripture, therefore, was only one of many sources of truth, and an imperfect one. Insights were sought and found in Plato, the supreme philosopher, and Homer, the inspirer of poets.[30] With Paul, these were the divinely inspired teachers of knowledge. All religious knowledge and experience was relevant to salvation, and through the Saviour Christ, this was now available to all capable of receiving it.

[28] *The Treatise on the Resurrection* 46, ed. J. Robinson, p. 52. Compare Theodotus, ed. Foerster, *Gnosis*, 41:2. The Church was chosen "before the foundation of the world."

[29] The ideas of the Naassenes (People of the Serpent) in particular, cited by Hippolytus, *Refutatio* v:6.7, pp. 20-22.

[30] For Homer as "poet," see *inter alia The Exegesis on the Soul* 137:1, ed. J. Robinson, p. 186. Valentinus follows Plato and uses the term "demiourgos" for the Creator.

The Gnostic interpretation of Christianity, however, had little connection with the Biblical faith that was inspiring the Great Church. The Gnostics regarded the Scriptural narrative as fit for simpletons, just as they regarded the ceremonies of the Church as "material," honouring the Creator, and not God.[31] The tone and content of their literature was a thousand miles removed from that of the Gospels. The life and ministry of Christ had little place in their systems. Christ was "the divine messenger," the "bringer of knowledge" sent from God, the Father of All, to enable his hearers to "know themselves," illumine the hidden light within them, wake them from slumber and fit themselves for salvation. Christ's stay on earth was the stay of a heavenly being united temporarily with a mortal, which was ended at the Passion. The powers of evil responsible for the Crucifixion had destroyed a man, not Christ.[32]

Behind this view of Christ lay a radically dualistic view of reality. It assumed an insuperable division and antagonism between God and the divine world that He had brought into being and the world that surrounded humanity. That world had come about through a series of catastrophes through which the harmony of the divine world had been compromised and an imperfect universe created, ruled over by malevolent beings, the chief of which was the God of the Jews. In each individual, however, dwelt a self or soul that belonged to the divine world, as did truth and knowledge itself, but had become drugged with slumber and imprisoned in the world around us.[33] It could be freed only by accepting the call of the Saviour Christ, but in most cases the influence of the servants of the creator of this world, and the planetary deities that controlled time and hence the destiny of individuals, was too strong. Those who remained earth-bound were destined to Error (*Plané*) and Oblivion.

---

[31] Heracleon, cited in Origen, *Comment. in Johannem* xiii:19, and see E. Pagels, "A Valentinian Interpretation of Baptism and the Eucharist," *Harvard Theological Review* 65 (1972), pp. 162-169.

[32] Irenaeus, *Adv. Haer.* 1:24.4.

[33] *Gospel of Truth* 29-30, ed. J. Robinson, p. 43.

Not surprisingly, the organisation of the Gnostic communities was non-ecclesiastical. Their leaders were teachers, their religious life resembled that of contemporary adherents of the mystery sects. Liturgies were spiritual. In the Eucharist, for instance, they gave thanks to the Father remembering for the sake of Christ (his message of salvation?) and rejoicing in those who "are complete in every spiritual gift and (every) purity."[34] There was no idea of sacrifice, or any connection between Eucharist and imitation of Christ's death through martyrdom. There were also final instructions to the dying, how to outwit the powers that would try to prevent the upward flight of the soul.[35] Secrecy, ability to protect their saving message until the end, and not its open confession was the aim of the Gnostic believer.[36]

Such were some of the tenets of this new generation of interpreters of Christ's message. Prominent among these were, according to Origen in the next century, Alexandrian Greeks.[37] The claim is significant, for mutual amalgamation between Judaism and Hellenism had taken place in Alexandria as nowhere else in the ancient world. Alexandrian Jews like Alexandrian Greeks were tending to understand God in Platonic terms, as Existence that had neither beginning nor end, and who had created the divine world, "out of nothing,"[38] and whom man could only apprehend through the intermediary creative power of His Wisdom or Word, though the Gnostic Christ plays a more direct part as agent of human salvation than Philo's Word. This could in turn be equated to the Platonic *Nous* (Mind), and the angels with the Platonic Ideas. Such speculation leading to the depreci-

---

[34]Valentinian Exposition on the Eucharist, ed. Robinson, p. 442.

[35]For the followers of Marcus among the Gallic Gnostic Christians, cited by Irenaeus, *Adv. Haer.* 1:21.5.

[36]Irenaeus, *Adv. Haer.* 1:24.6, and Epiphanius, *Panarion* xxiv:5.4, concerning Basilides and his followers.

[37]Origen, *Contra Celsum* iii:12.

[38]Philo, *Mos.* ii:267. See G. May, *Schöpfung aus dem Nichts* (Berlin/New York, 1978), p. 16.

ation of Jahweh, the Creator God of the Old Testament, made Alexandria a natural centre for the Gnostic movement within Christianity.

Until the discovery of the Gnostic library of 52 treatises at Nag Hammadi not far from Luxor in Egypt, Gnostic beliefs had to be assessed mainly from the work of the Church Fathers. Of the most important were Irenaeus (flor. 185-195), Clement of Alexandria (flor. 180-200), and Hippolytus of Rome (flor. 210-230). Only eight complete Gnostic works were known, and of these two remained unpublished. The discovery of the jar containing the papyrus codices by peasants digging fertiliser in December 1945 has deepened (though not altered fundamentally) a scholar's understanding of Gnosticism. How and why it took 32 years from the discovery until Professor J. M. Robinson's publication of the Nag Hammadi documents in English, for a full edition to be completed, has been told brilliantly by John Dart in his book *The Laughing Savior*.[39] Here, it suffices to say, the French official career-structure which diverted the gifted young Jean Doresse from Coptic to Ethiopic studies, the wars in the Middle East, elements of scholarly selfishness and institutional caution, and the requirement of lengthy negotiations between antique dealers who possessed the codices and the Egyptian government that wanted to exert their legal rights over them, all conspired to prevent their study by scholars. Then it was largely due to the inspiration of Professor Robinson that the work of coordination, edition and translation went forward.

The Nag Hammadi documents confirm the fervent Christianity of the Gnostics. In no way was it related to the Christianity of the Gospels, but in no way did its adherents intend to build bridges with current philosophy. "A heathen man does not die," proclaimed the *Gospel of Philip*, "for he has never lived that he should die. The believer is only alive since Christ came."[40] Judaism was regarded as a sort of halfway house between the folly of paganism and the truth

---

[39] *The Laughing Savior,* part i (New York, 1976).
[40] *The Gospel of Philip* 52, ed. Robinson, p. 132.

which the Gnostics possessed. "In the days that we were Hebrews, we were orphans. We had (only) our mother, but when we became Christians we acquired father and mother" from the same Gospel.[41] Heracleon (c. 175) makes the same point, but accuses ordinary (orthodox) Christians of "worshipping as Jews," in "celebrating the Jewish Passover in the Eucharist."[42]

Yet, the treatises from the library show how permeated by Judaism the Gnostics were. One can see how Jewish speculations on different Creation narratives told in the Book of Genesis and the prophecies of Daniel formed basic elements in the Gnostic systems. Jerusalem too, though no longer a Jewish city in the second century, continued to exercise its attraction. Jewish metaphors such as "a high-priestly garment" as the equivalent of wisdom and understanding came naturally to the writers (*Teaching of Silvanus*, Robinson, p. 349). Another example, the *Secret Teaching of John*, of which three copies were found in the library, reflects the ideas of Valentinus and his school. This sets the scene of the Apostle John's vision of the secrets of the Beyond, in the wilderness not far from Jerusalem. John, the brother of James, meets a Pharisee called Ananias on the steps of the Temple. Ananias upbraids him. "Where is your Master whose disciple you were? You followed a deceiver who estranged you from the tradition of your fathers," i.e., the presumption was that the Gnostic was an apostate Jew.[43] Indeed, down to the end of the second century, this was how Christianity appeared to many educated pagans.[44] With the Gnostics, their angelology, their preoccupation with the planets and the zodiac, and the use of the name of Jahweh, indicate how much, despite its Platonism, the newly perfected Christianity still owed to the Old Israel.

Our information on the personalities of the Gnostic leaders indicates the movement as one of transition from a

---

[41] *Ibid.*

[42] Heracleon, Frag. 22, cited by Origen, *Comment. in Johannem* xiii:19.

[43] *The Secret Teaching of John*, ed. Robinson, p. 99.

[44] Origen, *Contra Celsum* ii:2 and 4.

predominantly Jewish to a predominantly Gentile religion. We do not know who were the predecessors in Alexandria of *Basilides*, but it is difficult to think that the system which he and his son Isidore elaborated had no previous representatives. They themselves symbolize the transition that characterizes second century Christianity. In the quarter of a century, between 125-150, in which they flourished, they achieved an enormous amount. Basilides wrote 24 books of scriptural exegesis, the first recorded Christian commentary on either Septuagint or Gospels; his son produced a book of ethics and a work on prophecy called *The Exposition of the Prophet Pachor*.[45] Together they ranged through theology, morals, exegesis, and mysticism, discussing the relations between God and creation, the possibility of sin in Jesus, the ethics of martyrdom, the cause of human suffering and the prospect of reincarnation. Basilides attempted a philosophy of religion centered on Christ, but drawing from both pagan and Jewish sources, and reflecting also some of the problems of the day. Alexandria had suffered in the Jewish uprising of 115, and Basilides castigated Jahweh as an aggressive deity and the Jews as a people who took after him, aspiring to subjugate other nations.[46] Yet, like his contemporaries, such as the Alexandrian (?) writer of the *Letter* of Pseudo-Barnabas, his outlook was basically Jewish. For him, as for contemporary Jews, including Paul, ignorance was the characteristic feature of all unillumined Beings, whether men or deities. Of the latter, each of the 365 that came between God and creation believed himself to be the Supreme God.[47] For him, too, martyrdom was a form of atonement, as it was interpreted by the writer of 4 Maccabees, but in Basilides' system it was no longer a contribution to the collective salvation of the Jewish people, but one means by which the individual soul might hasten on its journey towards perfection.

[45]Clement of Alexandria, *Stromata* vi:6.53.2.

[46]Basilides, quoted by Irenaeus, *Adv. Haer.* 1:24.4.

[47]*Ibid.*, 1:24.5, and compare *On the Origin of the World* 100, ed. Robinson, p. 163.

Basilides was influenced positively by Plato. He is the first known Christian thinker who attempted to harmonise Platonism and Christianity, and to regard the salvation offered by the latter as attainable by methods similar to those used by a philosopher to approach his goal of truth. Basilides saw Christianity in terms of progression, whereby the disciple moved through paganism and Judaism to Christianity, which, however, only a few who had attained "knowledge of all things," would achieve. He cited the Second Book of the *Republic* to demonstrate that Providence was not, nor could be, the author of suffering and evil, and that apparently undeserved suffering could result from the existence of sinfulness as part of creation, or even from sins committed in a previous life.[48] The attempt, however, to explain sin and suffering on the basis that sinfulness was inherent in creation led Basilides towards a dualistic view of the universe; for if Providence was not the author of suffering, evil itself must be considered to have an independent existence. For Basilides, dualism was not an *a priori* assumption, but the unavoidable result of a theology of suffering and, indeed, of martyrdom.

Basilides had studied Genesis and come to radically different conclusions from his orthodox contemporaries. There is a serious difference of view concerning Basilides' cosmology between Irenaeus and Hippolytus, but both agree that he held the opinion uncompromisingly that the world was created "from nothing" and not from unformed matter as a literal reading of the first verse of Genesis suggests.[49] To cite Hippolytus' version: "Whence," he (Basilides) asks, "'came the light (Gen 1:3)? From nothing. For it has not been written,' he says, whence, but only from the voice of him who speaks the word, and he who speaks the word, he says, was non-existent."[50] Basilides was stressing the absolute transcendence of God, who created the cosmic

---

[48]Republic ii:579, cited in Clement, *Stromata* iv:12.81.1-3.

[49]Hippolytus, *Refutatio* vii:20.2.

[50]*Ibid.*, vii 22:3. See G. May, *op. cit.*, pp. 68-71.

seeds which contained in themselves the forces that in turn created the world. Christ was the Mind (*nous*), the first emanation from the Father, descending through the spheres in what can best be described as three stages, finally to rest upon Jesus the son of Mary. Thus, Jesus was enlightened by the light that shone upon him.

Christ therefore was a purely spiritual being, temporarily encased in a body, who had been sent by the Father to liberate mankind from Jahweh and his angels. The Gospels taught, Basilides claimed, quoting 1 Corinthians 2:13, "not in words taught of human wisdom but in those taught of the Spirit,"[51] and hence a purely spiritual message, instructing the Great Archon as to his nature as a begotten being and causing his repentance as well as teaching the Gnostic Christian. Thus, enlightenment and harmony would replace ignorance and disorder as characteristic of the universe.[52]

The progress of the spiritual being, the Gnostic believer, led to liberation of the soul and participation in the salvation of the universe itself. Basilides' disciples had no means, however, of regarding Christ as a personal saviour. All salvation took place in the realm of the spirit. Christ himself moved in a series of transfigurations, appearing to those who heard him in an appropriate form. To the Jews who attempted to kill him, he put away his body, and as he could not suffer, stood by and laughed at them (a reminiscence of Ps 59:8, "But thou, O Lord, shalt laugh at them: thou shalt have all the heathen in derision"). Simon of Cyrene was crucified in his place.[53] The true Christian, therefore, could not confess "the crucified Christ" but must seek identification with the spiritual Aeon that was the real Christ, and Scripture must be understood as unveiling the supernatural, the mysteries of creation.

On any criterion, Basilides was a bold and original thinker. The fragmentary and discordant character of our sources prevents us from judging whether the seeming con-

---

[51]*Ibid.*, vii:26.2.
[52]*Ibid.*, 27:1-3.
[53]Irenaeus, *Adv. Haer.*, 1:24.2.

tradictions in his thought, particularly as regards his cosmology, were real or not. The transcendence of God does not harmonise with the independence of evil nor the return of "enormous ignorance" at the end of time with the punishment of all creation. Were there two independent aspects of Basilides' thought, or does he bring them together in a work that has not survived? Nevertheless, the attempt at a Christian theology based both on detailed study of Scripture and current Platonism was a pioneering endeavor. When he began to teach in c. 130, Christianity was dominated still by materialist views of heaven and hell, of unimaginable blessings for the saved and equally horrendous tortures for the damned, described by bishops such as Papias of Hierapolis, or by writers such as the author of the *Preaching of Peter.* Basilides offered educated Christians a new prospect, without complete surrender to current philosophy, in a system that attempted to find clues to the problems of evil and suffering while offering hope of progress towards salvation for the illumined soul. In contrast to orthodox Christianity, enquiry rather than acceptance of tradition became the hall-mark of Gnosticism. By the end of the century, "Ask and it shall be given you" (Mt 7:2), Tertullian claimed, was their favorite text.[54] Thanks to Basilides and Isidore, this was the case.

As the second century wore on, the relationship between Scripture and the philosophy and ethics of the pagan world moved increasingly into the centre of debate between Gnostic and Orthodox. In circa 170, a remarkable letter was written by Ptolemy, one of Valentinus' disciples, probably in Rome. His correspondent was a lady called Flora, typical perhaps of the educated but under-occupied women of the period who found an outlet for their intellectual powers in the study and practice of mystery religion.[55] The Jewish Scriptures contained several layers of material, Ptolemy

---

[54]Tertullian, *De Praescriptione* 8.

[55]Text preserved by Epiphanius, *Panarion* xxxiii:3-7, commented upon by G. Quispel, *Ptolemée, Lettre à Flora* in *Sources Chrétiennes* (= *SG*) 24 (Paris, 1949). Partial English translation in J. Stevenson, *A New Eusebius*, pp. 91-95.

claimed. The Law contained in the Pentateuch had not been proclaimed all at the same time or by a single author. The Ten Commandments were God's Law but had been completed by the Sermon on the Mount.[56] Other prescriptions such as "eye for an eye" were abolished by the Saviour as they merely substituted one injustice for another. They were the work of an inferior God, not indeed evil, but concerned only with retributive justice, and could not be reconciled with the nature and goodness of the Father of All.[57] The various requirements in Scripture such as fasting and observing the Sabbath could be interpreted as types of prefigurations of laws laid down by the Saviour, and so the Old Testament was the product of "an Intermediate Being, a distant image of the Father, but ignorant of the Father's existence." Basilides and his followers would have agreed. This was a serious attempt to explain the existence of an imperfect universe governed by an imperfect Law, that had now the means of restoring its image through the coming of Christ.

The Gnostic legacy should not be underestimated. In Alexandria, many of the questions Origen asked, and much of his effort to understand the true meaning of the Fourth Gospel were reactions to Gnostic teaching. The *Commentary on John* could not have been written without Heracleon's pioneering work. It would seem also from the relations between the Nag Hammadi's library and the Pachomian monastery of Chenoboskion that it influenced more than is usually accepted the ethic of the Pachomian ascetic communities.[58] It contributed, in addition, to the popular piety of the eastern churches. Legends concerning the Virgin, including her Assumption begin in a Gnostic environment. This is true also of the Birth Narratives of Jesus. When one looks at the frescoes of the medieval Orthodox Church, one finds the scenes of the Birth of Christ taken less from the New Testament than from Gnostic legends (espe-

[56]Epiphanius, *Panarion* xxxiii:5.

[57]*Ibid.*, 7:4.

[58]See J. Robinson's comments, *op. cit.*, pp. 15-20, on this possibility.

cially from the *Proto-evangelium of James*) that elaborate the role of Joseph and Anna and their families. Gnosticism romanticised Christianity, contributed to its emancipation from Jewish Law, and directed it irreversibly towards the Gentile world.

Finally, may I come to an individual Christian leader who was neither a Gnostic nor an Alexandrian, but whose ideas led to some of the same conclusions as theirs.

Marcion was a contemporary of Basilides, but he was born at Sinope on the Black Sea coast, c. 90 A.D. His was a Christian merchant family and his father was "bishop" of the local community and another striking example of the post-Pauline mission in Asia Minor.[59] The environment in which he grew up saw strong rivalries between Christianity and Judaism, amid a suspicious provincial pagan population. The young Marcion was interested in philosophy as well as maintaining the family business. Like his Gnostic contemporaries, he felt that the key to understanding the universe and its relation to God was the problem of evil. How did this imperfect world come into being? How could the individual achieve salvation from it? From this questioning it would seem that Paul must have influenced him from the outset, for he never elaborated a speculative allegorical exegesis like the Gnostics. His conclusions on Law and Grace pushed Paul to the extremes and were apparently sufficiently shocking to provoke Polycarp of Smyrna to denounce him as "the first-born of Satan" before c. 135.[60] This incident was remembered long after in c. 185, by Irenaeus writing *Against the Heresies* far off in Lyons on the Rhone.

Like many of his contemporaries with similar interests Marcion emigrated to Rome c. 138. He was accepted by the Christians there, donated the community the relatively large sum of 200,000 sesterces, but came under the influence of a

---

[59]Justin Martyr, *1 Apol.* 1:26, Irenaeus, *Adv. Haer.* 1:25.1, and Tertullian, *Adv. Marcionem* 1:1, for Marcion's Pontic background.

[60]Irenaeus, *Adv. Haer.* 3:3.4.

Syrian Gnostic named Cerdo.[61] Cerdo seems to have sharpened the implicit dualism in Marcion's ideas, confirming him in his opinion that the God who spoke through the Law and the prophets was not the Father of Jesus Christ, for that deity had made himself known, whereas the Father on whom Jesus had called was not known. There were therefore two gods, the God of the Old Testament who represented the Law and its primitive ideas of justice and righteousness, and God, the Father, who was good.

Marcion is likely to have been aided in reaching this conclusion by a different route, namely through a study of Scripture and in particular the key work in the early Church, Second Isaiah. There, reading Isaiah 45:7, he found the claim made by Jahweh, "I make peace, and it is I who make evil. I the Lord do these things."[62] This became fundamental to his interpretation of Christianity, for, as he reminded his hearers, an evil tree could not bring forth good fruit. Moreover, Jahweh's acts bore out his statement. The morality of Jewish Scripture was alien to the teaching of the New Testament. Elisha had been permitted to vent his annoyance on children who teased him by having them eaten by bears (2 Kings 2:24).[63] Jesus had told his disciples to "suffer little children to come unto me and forbid them not" (Lk 18:16). He had stopped the sun in its path to allow Joshua to finish off the Amalekites (Jos 10:13). Jesus, through Paul, had said, "Let not the sun go down on your wrath" (Eph 4:26).[64] He was so ignorant that he did not know where Adam was in the Garden of Eden, and his harshness was demonstrated by laws of retribution.[65] The promises of the Creator were earthly and indeed military, while those of Christ were "not of this world" and heavenly.

The basis of Marcion's argument rejecting Jahweh as

---

[61]*Ibid.,* 1:27.1-3.

[62]Tertullian, *Adv. Marcionem* 1:2.2.

[63]*Ibid.,* 4:23.4-5.

[64]Megethius, cited by Adamantius, *Dialogues* 1:13.

[65]Tertullian, *Adv. Marcionem* 4:16. See A. von Harnack, *Marcion: das Evangelium vom fremden Gott* (Leipzig, 1921), pp. 104-106.

God had already been laid in Judaism. One of the Nag Hammadi documents was called the *Apocalypse of Adam*.[66] It had no Christian themes, but taught that the Creator-God who made the natural order was not God, and that Adam himself had a greater power than he, only that in the Fall he and Eve lost their Glory and knowledge and become enslaved to the Creator and subject to death. Adam, however, was illumined by powers sent from God and this illumination would enable other mortals to gain knowledge of God and live forever.

Marcion therefore was not the first to separate the Creator from God. His originality lay in suggesting that the "Unknown God" of Acts 17:23 was the Father of Jesus Christ recognised by Paul; he accepted Paul as the sole reliable interpreter of the message of Christ, and then he rejected the Old Testament en bloc together with the idea of a Jewish military and political Messiah. The true Messiah, Jesus, was sent by God to the human race to save souls, and coming from the world beyond, was revealed "as a man but not a man," a body only in appearance, not subject to weakness, passion or death.[67] Tertullian was for once being fair when he summed up Marcion's message. "Marcion laid down the position that Christ, who in the reign of Tiberius was, by a previously unknown God, revealed for the salvation of all nations, is a different being from him who was ordained by God the Creator for the restoration of the Jewish state, and who is yet to come. Between these, he interposes a separation of a great and absolute difference, as great as lies between what is just and what is good, as great as lies between the law and the gospel, as great as is the difference between Christianity and Judaism" (*Adv. Marcioniem* iv:6). For Marcion, Law and grace were not compatible.

Marcion deserved the grudging praise of Clement of Alexandria at the end of the second century, as well as the

---

[66]Robinson, *op. cit.*, pp. 156-164.

[67]*Adv. Marcionem*, 3:8, and compare *ibid.*, 4:8, Christ a "phantom."

opposition of every orthodox thinker of note.[68] In his own way he was as revolutionary as Basilides. He was the first to try to create a Christian canon of Scripture to mark the reality of Christians as the new people of God. Luke's Gospel from chapter three onwards (i.e., excluding the Birth narrative), and the ten Pauline epistles contained God's message through Christ and his interpreter Paul. Like Paul himself, he saw the threat to Christianity in the "Judaisers" who would thrust Christians back to the domination of the Creator-God. Hence, all references to the "promises of Abraham," to "flaming fire" and rewards and punishment were excised. The remainder was "the good news," God's uncovenanted gift to man, to be preached as Paul had set out to do, from one end of the inhabited world to the other.[69]

Marcion's views proved too much for the Roman community. In c. 144 he was expelled, and his donation returned to him. He spent the last decade or so of his life as a Christian missionary, following once more in Paul's footsteps. He planted churches, like "wasps make nests," Tertullian said of him. His heretical tradition "filled the whole world."[70] Rome, Carthage, and Nicomedia in Bithynia had Marcionite congregations, and more important than these even, were the communities established in eastern Syria where Marcion's became the majority religion of the inhabitants.[71] These churches were organised on a hierarchal basis, unlike some of the Gnostics, and Marcion's followers proclaimed their message, were ready to suffer martyrdom,[72] seeking no hidden meanings from Scripture and harbouring no secrets to be revealed only at the Last Day. They followed

---

[68] Beginning with Justin Martyr in his *First Apology*, 1:26, circa 155, and continued through Irenaeus, Tertullian, Clement of Alexandria, and Hippolytus.

[69] For instance, Tertullian, Adv. *Marcionem* 4.1ff.

[70] *Adv. Marcionem* 4:5.

[71] One of the earliest Christian inscriptions, dated to 318/319 from Lebaba in Syria records the existence of a Marcionite "synagogue," Dessau, *OGIS* 608. See also Walter Bauer, *Orthodoxy and Heresy in Earliest Christianity*, pp. 16-36.

[72] For instance, the example quoted by Eusebius in the Valerian persection, *H.E.* vii:12.1.

the word of the Gospel literally by preaching abandonment of the world, and granting full membership only to those prepared to lead an ascetic and abstinent life.[73] This was the first attempt to create a "gathered Church," on the basis of the literal acceptance of Christ's commands as preserved in their canon of Scripture. Significantly, it was in the rural areas of eastern Syria that they gained most adherents.

The Gnostics and Marcion's followers show two distinct, but allied aspects of the impact of Christianity in the second century. They reveal some of the questions those attracted to Christianity were asking. What was the meaning of creation? How was Christ's passion and death to be understood? What was the value of martyrdom and the meaning of suffering? Surely the religious insights of Plato and Homer were as relevant as those of Moses? They also reveal fervour of religious feeling and intellectual inquiry of the time. If they rejected the world as the world of the Creator, they were not necessarily pessimists and drop-outs. Opponents admitted the enthusiasm which the Gnostics and Marcion aroused among their followers. New truths were discovered daily; organisation was freed from institutional shackles.[74] There was an intellectual curiosity that was lacking among the orthodox and a sense of mission one misses among the latter in the mid-second century. Both movements, however, failed. For the Gnostics, their diffuseness was largely to blame. Individual enthusiasm could not compensate for a lack of permanent organisation. For the Marcionites, the insistence on uncompromised integrity and a ritual purity condemned them to the life of a small if respected sect. Even their lack of philosophical interest stood in the way of a successful universal appeal.[75] Moreover, the Jewish legacy could not be abandoned so easily, and the attempt by the Gnostics to replace the Old Testament with snatches of Plato and Homer was futile. Ultimately, while the Gnostics

---

[73]Tertullian, *Adv. Marcionem* 1:11. Marcionites "refused baptism except to the celibate or eunuch."

[74]Thus, Tertullian, *De Praese.* and Irenaeus, *Adv. Haer.*, 1.18.1.

[75]See Eusebius, *H.E.* v:13.5-7.

contributed to the background of the Alexandrian approach to the doctrines of the Trinity and the Person of Christ, and the Marcionites contributed to the ascetic tradition of Christianity, whether monastic or Manichee, it fell to the Great Church to provide the organisation and teaching that would eventually secure the triumph of new religion.

Source Material

Blackman, E. C., *Marcion and His Influence*. New York, 1950.

Bultmann, R., *Primitive Christianity in Its Contemporary Setting*. Philadelphia, 1980.

Cross, F. L., *The Jung Codex: A Newly Recovered Papyrus*. London, 1955.

Dart, J., *The Laughing Savior: The Discovery and Significance of the Nag Hammadi Gnostic Library*. New York, 1976.

Foerster W., *Gnosis: A Selection of Gnostic Texts*, 2 vols. London, 1972.

Grant, R. M., *Gnosticism and Early Christianity*. New York, 1966.

Jonas, Hans, *The Gnostic Religion*, 2nd. rev. ed., Boston, 1963.

Pagels, E., *The Gnostic Gospels*. New York, 1979.

Robinson, J. M., *The Nag Hammadi Library*. New York, 1978.

Rudolph, K., *Gnosis, the Nature and History of Gnosticism*. New York, 1983.

Wilson, R. McL., *The Gnostic Problem*. London, 1958.

3

Old Priest: New Prophet

Our knowledge of the Gnostic movement has been transformed by the archaeological revolution. In this we have noted the part played by the enterprise of the present generation of American scholars.

At this point we turn to the more prosaic aspects of the story of early Christianity, first, briefly, the orthodox reaction to Basilides, Valentinus and Marcion, how the Great Church tried to tackle the same intellectual problems that had faced the Gnostics, but, secondly, how from the progressive strengthening of the Church's organisation designed to confront the Gnostics and Marcion arose a new movement of dissent that was to have far-reaching repercussions, particularly in the western half of Christendom. The New Prophecy eventually inspired much of the Christianity of the new but immensely important North African Church.

The Gnostics had attacked either directly or by implication everything that the Great Church held dear, its concept of the reality of Christ's mission, its interpretation of baptism and the eucharist, the status of the clergy that served its liturgy, the validity of its Scriptures, its ideal of the imitation of Christ through martyrdom, and the literal understanding of the Coming, of Judgment and Paradise — all these fell under the Gnostic or Marcionite hammer.

Orthodox Christianity had to live in the same world as its opponents. It lacked, however, some of their advantages. Paul and his followers had linked pagan philosophy with pagan morals, "vain deceit after the tradition of men," (Col 2:8) and quite unreasonably attacked both. The pagan world was far from the cesspit of iniquity caricatured by first-century Christian writers. "Pietas" (religion) and "Pudicitia" (virtue and chastity) were shared by pagan and Christian alike as the ideals of the good life. Moreover, many members of Christian communities were as introspective and arrogant towards their neighbours as some sectaries today. About 178 A.D. an educated Greek provincial, probably living in Syria, wrote a tract against Christianity in which he describes the Christians he had encountered. They were like "frogs squatting around a marsh, discussing who was the most sinful among them," and comforting themselves with the thought that God had abandoned the rest of the world to its fate to devote himself entirely to the Christians![1]

This was unpromising soil for any fruitful contact with the Greco-Roman world, such as the the Gnostics were attempting. It was more difficult for the "saints" than the "sinners." Yet we find, contemporaneously with the Gnostic movement, Christians in the Great Church who were attempting to combine acceptance of their Jewish heritage with assertions that harmony with the pagan world was not impossible.

Between 125-190, these *Apologists*, as they were called, attempted first to defend Christianity against charges of atheism and black magic that were circulating among the Greco-Roman provincials, and secondly to present a philosophic defence of the religion on different and more orthodox lines from those used by the Gnostics.

It is not an accident that we find the first known orthodox scriptural exegesis that of Justin in his write-up of his *Dialogue with Trypho*, circa 160, almost exactly contemporary

---

[1]Origen, *Contra Celsum* iv:23.

with that of the Gnostics.[2] This, however, belongs to the continued "dialogue" between orthodoxy and Judaism and the establishment of Christians as "God's new people." Here we are concerned more with the relations between the Church and the pagan world. Our first witness is, inconveniently enough, not dated except rather vaguely to circa 150, the writer of an anonymous tract addressed to a certain *Diognetus*.

Orthodox apologetic is the heir to the Jewish critique of paganism, examples of which can be found in Psalm 115:2ff., the Book of Wisdom, and the Third (Jewish) Sibylline Oracle. Thus, like his Jewish predecessors, the Christian writer castigates his pagan contemporaries as "ignorant," worshipping God's creation and not God, that their idols were dumb and lifeless, helpless against the daily hazards of wind and weather. The Christians, however, represented mankind before God — one is reminded of similar claims made by Philo on behalf of the Jews a century before, and in a well-known passage, the writer claimed, also in the spirit of universalist Judaism, that "broadly speaking, what the soul is in the body, the Christians are in the world. The soul dwells in the body, but it is not the body, and the Christians dwell in the world but are not of the world."[3] They were the leaven, accepting as their lot the hatred of Jew and pagan, but bearing witness to the love of God for his creation. The Christian Gospels fulfilled the predictions of the Jewish prophets, and the Church was pursuing its way on a "free exulting course."[4] Far from repudiating the Jewish heritage, the writer was asserting the divine character of the Old Testament, but only the (orthodox) Christians interpreted it aright and were the heirs to its promises. The anonymous writer laid down the lines of argument his orthodox colleagues were to use in their conflict with paganism, Gnosticism and the followers of Marcion. His younger

[2] Dating, see L. W. Barnard, *Justin Martyr: His Life and Thought* (Cambridge, 1967), p. 23.

[3] *Ep. ad Diognetum* vi:1.

[4] *Ibid.*, xi:6.

contemporary, Justin, widened the scope of his arguments and showed, even in a muddle-headed way, how orthodox Gentile Christianity was destined to develop in the Greek-speaking provinces of the empire.

Justin (circa 100-165) was a good example of the dissatisfaction felt by many lettered provincials with the state of religion of the time, represented by the philosophies and philosophers. He tells us himself of his long odyssey through Stoicism, the Peripatetics, the Pythagoreans, the Academics to the Platonists where for some time he felt himself at home. He believed himself, as he said, "near the vision of God."[5] A chance encounter with an old but alert and well-read Christian on the sea shore near Ephesus jolted his self-confidence. The soul could not remember experiences of a previous existence. Only the Hebrew prophets had foretold the process of human salvation accurately when they prophesied concerning Christ he said, but the intellectual argument did not convince Justin entirely.[6] As he said, it was the sight of the martyrs with their fearless bearing that converted him,[7] and thenceforth he wore his philosopher's cloak as portending that of a "Christian philosopher."[8]

In the 150s the Christians were becoming as unpopular as the Jews had been in the cities of western Asia Minor a century or so before. They were suspected not only of being clannish and disloyal to both the gods and emperors but also of being in league with malevolent powers and dabbling in black magic.[9] Incest and cannibalism were not merely private vices, but were of so horrific a character that they could bring upon a community that tolerated them the

[5] *Dialogue with Trypho*, 2:7.

[6] See the very perceptive account by R. E. Grant concerning the record of Justin's spiritual odessey and especially his encounter with the ancient Christian at Ephesus, *Augustus to Constantine* (London, 1971), pp. 110-112.

[7] *II Apology* 12.

[8] *Dialogue* 1.

[9] For the popular charges against the Christians in the second century, often believed by educated provincials, see Fronto quoted in Minucius Felix, *Octavius* 9:6 and 31:2, Eusebius, *H.E.* v:1.14 (martyrs of Lyon), Justin, *I Apol.* 5, and Athenagoras, *Plea*, 1-3.

anger of the gods in the form of natural disasters.[10] Provincials from Gaul to Carthage and Rome and Asia Minor believed this, and their resultant anger at the Christians was the main cause of persecution during the second century. Justin denied these charges,[11] and his rebuttal of their even more damaging accusation of "atheism" enabled him to put the Christian case in the form of an open letter to the emperor, but in fact offered to public opinion. He claimed that Christ was the revelation of God, acting on creation like the Seminal Word of the Stoics, and whose force therefore had enlightened mankind throughout the ages.[12] Thus, one reached the rather astonishing conclusion that all that had been good and valuable in the past, whether in truths proclaimed by poets and philosophers or in the utterances of the Old Testament prophets, was implicitly Christian. Abraham and Socrates were both "Christians before Christ."[13] With the coming of Christ, however, God's Word had become fully revealed and hence Christ's followers participated in his revelation more completely than the Jewish and Greek sages before him. To Justin, then, Christianity was identical with what was reasonable, and its enemies were forces of unreason inspired by demons (1 *Apology* 57). In addition, claimed Justin, the Hebrew prophets in the Old Testament had been in a special way vehicles of divine truth and they preceded the Greek poets in point of time. The latter had copied their ideas.[14] In the ancient world, the more ancient was the truer, for the further back in time one went, the greater had been access to religious truth and nearer to the golden age of Creation.

Justin thus presented orthodox Christians with an alter-

---

[10]For this attitude among the public in Carthage circa 190-200, see Tertullian's well-known comment (*Apol.* 40:2), "If the Tiber reaches the walls, if the Nile does not rise to the fields, if the sky does not move, or the earth does, if there is famine, if there is plague, the cry is at once, 'The Christians to the lion.' What, all of them to one lion!"

[11]*I Apol.* 5-7.

[12]*I Apol.* 46; compare *II Apol.* 13.

[13]*Ibid.*, 46, and compare *II Apol.* 10 — Christ and Socrates compared.

[14]*Ibid.*, 44 (Plato plagiarising Moses), and compare *ibid.*, 59-60.

native scheme of relations between Church and pagan society to that put forward by the Gnostics. Unlike the latter he had been able to find a role for philosophy while maintaining the primacy of Scripture and rejecting the pagan cultus. He was not, however, a consistent thinker. Like most theologians on the orthodox side, he believed strongly in the material joys of the Millennium, the reign of the saints,[15] while his association of Jesus Christ with the divine, creative power in the universe was arbitrary. Too many leaps of faith were required in his philosophy. As his Jewish opponent said of him, "the Christians tried to shape the Messiah for themselves and find texts to fit their fancy," and even those were at best ambiguous, "containing nothing decisive for his (Justin's) arguments."[16] And typically major arguments ranged over the precise rendering of Isaiah 7:14. Was it "Behold, a young woman shall conceive," or "Behold, a virgin shall conceive," as Justin affirmed. Not surprisingly his Jewish opponent told him that he would have done better to have remained a Platonist philosopher.[17]

All this, however, was not in vain. Justin had been able to show that it was possible to combine Platonism and Christianity without being a Gnostic. It was bold, at least, to attempt to harmonize the philosophies of the day with the Hebrew prophets and Plato with the Millennium, and then to go on to assert that the Old and New Testaments formed a self-consistent whole concerned only with the Messiah whom the Christians acknowledged. Orthodox Christianity was the true religion, the only means of interpreting the universe in terms of an harmonious creation in which the emperor and his servants had their due place. The enemies were demons, forces of unreason, who dwelt in idols and inspired their lying worship and even mimicry of Christian rites.[18]

[15] *Dialogue* 80:2 and 5. (Jerusalem would be physically rebuilt during that time.)

[16] *Dialogue* 51:1. Compare 39:3. Justin's exegesis showed that he "was out of his mind."

[17] *Ibid.*, 8:3.

[18] *I Apol.* 66. Compare, for alleged Mithraic imitation of Christian communion, Tertullian, *De Praescriptione* 40 (written circa 200 A.D.).

Justin shows that "the saints" were beginning to take the offensive. This did not end with his martyrdom in Rome in 165. A dozen years later one finds another Christian writer even more intent than Justin had been to demonstrate that orthodox Christianity was both true and beneficial to the empire. *Athenagoras* (circa 177) indeed flatters the emperors whom he is addressing, referring to them as "excelling all others in intelligence and in piety toward the true God."[19] They had established justice and harmony throughout the empire and peace for the cities. And he accepted many of the social values of pagan society, including slave-holding.[20] For him, Christianity would be associated with the best of pagan society and was to be regarded as an entirely positive force on the side of the state. The Christian Platonist could never be a political rebel.

In the last quarter of the second century orthodoxy had built up a formidable intellectual defence against its rivals, whether pagan or sectarian. Against the latter, arguments based on tradition and the priority of orthodox traditions against heretical carried weight; and on the orthodox side were immensely long-lived representatives, such as Polycarp, who, in Rome circa 154, could tell his hearers just what orthodox tradition that he had from John of Ephesus, seventy years before, really was![21] The Church, whether consciously or not, was looking into the future and to its role in a Christian empire. In this, the social fabric of the state and its institutions would be defended, and, as Clement of Alexandria showed in his tract on "The Rich Man's Salvation," circa 190, the Lord's injunctions, as contained in the Gospels, would be adapted to the institutional interests of the Church and its members.[22]

This aspect of the Church's life was also developing. By about 175, the norm of Church government in all major

[19]Athenagoras, *Plea* 6. Compare *ibid.*, 7.

[20]*Ibid.*, 35.

[21]Irenaeus, *Adv. Haer.* iii:3.4.

[22]Clement of Alexandria, *The Rich Man's Salvation*, ed. G. W. Butterworth, 15:1-6.

urban communities had become the monarchical bishop. Lists of successions, some allegedly extending back to apostolic foundation, had been drawn up,[23] and a network of communications between see and see had become established throughout the eastern Mediterranean. Orthodox leaders show themselves as men of the same cultural background, using the same language, Greek, and with the same general interests of suppressing heresies and dampening down excesses of enthusiasm. In *Irenaeus* of Lyons (circa 130-circa 200) orthodoxy found a champion who combined a long life with a determined character, pungent turn of phrase, and a photographic memory, and whose influence on the formation of Catholic orthodoxy has been enormous.

There is no point here in engaging in the old debate whether Irenaeus was a "pioneer" or a "traditionalist." He was a bit of both, a widely travelled and perceptive individual who lived up to his name "Man of Peace" (Irenaeus= Solomon). For what it is worth, I think that he stood near to the Hellenistic-Jewish tradition, and like the rabbis of the early second century, he saw tradition as the hedge for the (Christian) law.[24]

He was born probably in Smyrna and stayed there long enough to carry throughout his life a vivid image of Polycarp the bishop and to remember him as the epitome of orthodoxy.[25] He was the presbyter to whom reference could constantly be made on matters of doctrinal and disciplinary orthodoxy later. Irenaeus may have gone to Rome and studied with Justin, but the only certain date is that he was a member of the Christian community at Lyons in Gaul in

[23]Hegesippus, cited by Eusebius, *H.E.* iv:20.5-8. See T. H. Klauser, "Die Anfänge der römischen Bischofsliste" (= pp. 121-128 of *Gesammelte Arbeiten zur Liturgiegeschite, Kirchengeschichte und christliche Archaeologie,* ed. E. Dasmann (Münster, 1974).

[24]For "tradition" as a "hedge for Torah," see Rabbi Akiba cited in "Sayings of the Fathers" (*Pirke Aboth*) 3:18, ed. R. H. Charles, *The Apocrypha and Pseudepigrapha of the Old Testament* (Oxford, 1913), p. 701. "Tradition" in this case meant a tradition of correct interpretation of the Law.

[25]Eusebius, *H.E.* v:20.5-8, and Irenaeus, *Adv. Haer.* iv:26.2 ("blessed presbyter").

177, escaped the pogrom through a temporary absence, and
was used by the arrested Christians there as a go-between
with Pope Eleutherus on the question of the orthodoxy or
otherwise of the New Prophecy or Montanist movement.[26]
In circa 178 he became bishop; a little later he began his
great, five-volume work *Against the Heresies*; in the 190s he
was again on a mission of peace to Rome, this time to plead
the course of forbearance and tolerance in the dispute over
the dating of Easter that threatened to divide the Roman see
from the Christians in Asia Minor.[27] His busy and productive life ended about 200 A.D.

By 180 there were Marcionite churches and Gnostic cells
among the Christians up and down the Mediterranean.[28]
Irenaeus was stung into action as a defender of orthodoxy
by the success of a Gnostic named Marcus among wealthy
female Christians belonging to his flock.[29] *Against the
Heresies* was aimed primarily against the Gnostics and Marcionites, and in the first book he came straight to the point in
defence of orthodoxy. Christianity, he claimed, was a faith
spoken with one voice, based on tradition handed down to
the Churches by the Apostles and accepted by the Christians
everywhere. The Rule of Faith that supported this statement declared that Christian belief was in "one God, the
Father Almighty, who made the heaven, the earth, and the
seas and all that was in them, and in one Jesus Christ, the
Son of God, who was made flesh for our salvation, and in
the Holy Spirit, who through the prophets proclaimed the
dispensations of God which included resurrection of the
body and Judgement."[30] This faith, he declared, was based
on the tradition of the Apostles handed down to the entire
world and "is guarded by the succession of elders for those
who wish to behold the truth."[31] There were no hidden

[26] Eusebius, *H.E.*, v:3.4.
[27] *Ibid.*, v:23.11-12.
[28] See above, pp. 54-55.
[29] *Adv. Haer.* i:13.
[30] *Ibid.*, i:10.1-12.
[31] *Ibid.*, iii:2.2

mysteries to which the Gnostics laid claim. The authority of the Bible sufficed. It was guaranteed by tradition.

Irenaeus had struck at his opponents where they were weakest, on the issue of authority. The uncertain succession of Gnostic *gnosis* was less credible than the ordered succession of Catholic bishops. In addition, he was prepared to give a reasonable answer to those, like Marcion, who claimed that the inconsistencies in the Old and New Testaments could only be explained by the former's being the record of actions of an inferior "creator God" from whom man was delivered by Jesus Christ. Irenaeus would have none of this. There was no contrast between "natural man" made by the "creator God" and spiritual man made by the Unknown God. Man was one: he had been originally made "a little lower than the angels," but through misuse of his free will at the Fall the original likeness of God in him had become obscured.[32] The "image," however, he retained. The story of mankind told in the two Testaments was the story of his gradual recovery of that "likeness." Each stage on the long way home was marked by Covenants; that of Noah, of Abraham and of Moses, and thence through the prophets to the manifestation of God through Christ.[33] Christ was the Pauline Second Adam, summing up all truth in himself and reversing step by step the sins and failings of Adam through his birth from a Virgin, obedience to his Father, his death and destruction of evil through the resurrection.[34]

The Bible therefore formed a single, consistent whole. Salvation was a process of education. Each Covenant had been for its time, but each had been superseded, just as Christianity had now superseded Judaism;[35] man himself was not the product of some evilly-disposed god, but had been made by God for a set purpose. His progress did not

[32]*Ibid.*, v:16.1:2. See Jean Daniélou, *The Gospel Message and Hellenistic Culture,* trans. J. A. Baker (London, 1973), pp. 398-408.

[33]*Ibid.*, iii:11.8; compare iv:24:2, 25:2 and 38.

[34]*Ibid.*, v:19:1.

[35]*Epideixis,* 96, ed. J. A. Robinson (London, 1920). Christians have "no need of the Law as a tutor."

depend on passing from the authority of one divine being to another, but of fearing God by worship and obedience.

It was indeed a coherent system, embracing a Christology and anthropology, the unity of Scripture, the authority of the Gospel-tradition, and the emergent power of the clergy. But a price was to be exacted. Irenaeus' theology depended wholly on the Bible, and its total inspiration. No allowance was made for difficult strata of tradition or levels of authority, such as Ptolemy had sought to establish. Philosophy also was deeply suspect to him. He had little time for that "ancient Athenian, Plato."[36] This single-minded approach to complex theological problems resulted in inflexibility and narrowness.[37] If the Gnostics were wrong, at least they stimulated intellectual inquiry, but if the faith was "ever one and the same," the scope for exploration was limited. Salvation depended on accepting set forms of belief, organisation, and worship. Moreover, if he could defeat Marcion on general principles, he would still have had to reconcile individual incidents, such as the slaughter of the Amalekites or David's adulterous career with the love and perfection of God. Irenaeus, however, did not argue such details. The horror with which he treated all forms of deviation, even to the extent of failing to describe the beliefs of one former friend Florinus to whom he writes in protest, boded ill for those who stepped beyond permitted orthodoxy.[38] Christianity threatened to become as legalistic as the Judaism it had repudiated. The "great questions," however, of life and conduct asked by the Gnostics and Marcion could not be answered and, according to Irenaeus, should never have been raised.[39]

---

[36]*Adv. Haer.* ii:33:2.

[37]See J. Daniélou, *op. cit.*, p. 257. "In this particular sector of theology (Trinitarian), it must be admitted that the Gnostics, even if bad theologians, are at any rate more of theologians than Irenaeus."

[38]Cited by Eusebius, *H.E.*, v. 20.

[39]For Irenaeus' limitation of the scope of human knowledge, see his indignant rejoinder to the Gnostic(?) or pagan questions, "What was God doing before he made the world?" *Adv. Haer.* ii:41:4.

Irenaeus has rightfully been considered the "first Catholic Father," and, indeed, his main ideas survived Reformation and Counter-Reformation until the Enlightenment swept aside the bounds he had placed on human inquiry. Perhaps even in his own day his work circulated throughout Christendom, in Egypt[40] as well as in Gaul. He reflected the ecclesiastical spirit of his day. In his lifetime the Church, interpreting a Rule of Faith through the medium of one language, Greek, and sustained by an organisation of likeminded individuals often in communication with each other, was as united as it ever has been before or since.

Division was to arise from a source that Irenaeus could have anticipated from his experience at Lyons, and with which he half-sympathised. The loophole that he left in this otherwise strongly authoritarian system of Church government was in prophecy.[41] Despite his hope of the ultimate "divinization" of the individual, Irenaeus was also a chiliast, that is, he believed in the Millennium of the Just, and indeed his description of the material joys of that state provides the climax to his five books against the heresies.[42] Prophecy, however, requires prophets, and an acknowledgment that the Holy Spirit would work through them as well as through the ordered hierarchy of the Church. In this, Irenaeus was saying no more than his fellow Christians of Lyons. When persecution had struck in 177, they had shown themselves in every whit convinced that the Last Days were approaching and that it was the Spirit that guided their defence against the authorities.[43] In conceding the continuing validity of prophecy, however, Irenaeus opened the door to an alternative doctrine of the Church and its ministry, a doctrine capable of undermining the system he had defended so ably.

---

[40] A papyrus fragment of Irenaeus' *Adv. Haereses* has been found at Oxyrhynchus, *Pap. Oxy.* iii:405.

[41] Adv. Haer. iii:11:9. Compare iv:33:15 for Irenaeus' association of prophecy with the Last Times, which he believed were at hand.

[42] *Adv. Haer.* v:28-36.

[43] Eusebius, *H.E.* v:1:10 (concerning Vettius Epagathus). See also Frend, *Martyrdom and Persecution in the Early Church* (Oxford, 1965), ch. 1.

The Spirit could not be subject to Tradition.

It had been only a decade previously, in circa 172, that Montanus, a one-time priest of Cybele and convert to Christianity in Phrygia, had suddenly begun to announce that the Coming was about to take place near the village of Pepuza, about fifteen miles west of the town of Philadelphia.[44] He was accompanied by two women prophetesses, and between them they proclaimed the approach of the Millennium, which was to be preceded, however, by wars, earthquakes, and other catastrophes.[45] They declared that the command of the Holy Spirit was for Christians to be ready to accept a martyr's death and to prepare for it by stringent fasts and abstinences.[46]

Why this movement should have surfaced at this moment is a matter of speculation — perhaps severe local persecutions were a primary cause — but whatever the cause, Montanus had reactivated a tradition of prophecy which in Phrygia had kept pace with the progress of episcopal Christianity.[47] The clergy felt themselves threatened and took fright. Their hands, however, were tied. They could not deny the continuous activity of the Spirit in the Church, nor the approach of the last times, nor the role of the prophet, and there was a good scriptural tradition of women prophetesses, beginning with Deborah and Rahab and including Anna (Luke 2:36). Their existence, however, was also resented as enemies of the priesthood whether in the Old or New Israel (cf. Nehemiah 6:14). Resentment surfaced. Every type of scurrilous accusation was heaped on the prophets and prophetesses and, in particular, that they prophesied "in the Spirit" or in ecstasy, not in an apparently normal frame of mind as indicated in the books of the

---

[44]Eusebius, *H.E.* v:16; Epiphanius, *Panarion* 48:1. Here I accept the dating of Eusebius' *Chronicon*. For the location of Pepuza, see W. M. Calder, "Philadelphia and Montanism," *Bull. of John Rylands Library* 7 (1923), pp. 309-355.

[45]Anonymous anti-Montanist writer cited by Eusebius, *H.E.* v:16:18.

[46]For Montanist emphasis on martyr deaths, see Eusebius, *H.E.* v:16:20, and for the necessity of fasting in order to receive the Spirit, Tertullian, *On Fasting* 9.

[47]Eusebius, *H.E.* v:17:2-3.

Israelite prophets.[48]

There were, of course, answers. The Montanists claimed that the disciples "knew not what they said" at the moment of the Transfiguration,[49] but the bishops of the Great Church made it abundantly clear that it had little use for prophets and especially for prophetesses. In circa 179, one of these, Maximilla, lamented, "I am driven as a wolf from the sheep. I am not a wolf. I am word, spirit, and power."[50]

Alas, for her, the clergy gradually gained the upper hand, but with two far-reaching exceptions. First, the New Prophecy took root in the Phrygian countryside where it was to remain in being as a separate Church for generations. Second, it found adherents among the first known generation of Christians in North Africa. At this point the archaeologist begins to make his contribution to the study of Church history.

From the last twenty years of the nineteenth century, scholars from Western Europe, from Germany, France, Austria and Britain have explored western Asia Minor in search of epigraphic evidence of life there under the Roman Empire. Some outstanding remains of early Christianity, such as the two inscriptions relating to the Christian traveller Abercius, have been found, [51] and among these have been inscriptions relating to Montanism.

The Tembris valley in northern Phrygia was the site of an extensive imperial state. In 1923 W. M. Calder published a series of inscriptions he had found there. These were dated between 249 and 279 and had been set up by Christians who proclaimed their faith for all to see. They included the formula "Christians for Christians" and characterised the

---

[48] *Ibid.*, v:17:21.

[49] Unfortunately, Tertullian's *De Ecstasi*, in which he defended the Montanist position, no longer exists, but Athenagoras, *Plea* 9, takes it as a matter of course that a prophet would be simply the vehicle of the Spirit.

[50] Eusebius, *H.E.*, v:16:17.

[51] For the Abercius inscription, see W. M. Ramsay, *Cities and Bishoprics in Phrygia*, ii, 722-725, and for a recent scholarly commentary by E. Wischmeyer, "Die Aberkiosinschrift als Grabepigramm," *JAC* 23 (1980), pp. 22-47.

deceased in glowing, militant terms, in one case as "a soldier" (of Christ).[52] There was no attempt at concealment, no guarded use of "neutral" terminology to confuse the suspicious as to the allegiance of him who was commemorated. While it has now been argued that these stones need not all be Montanist,[53] some use known Montanist formulae, and none has been found in an indubitably Catholic setting. Moreover, they were not the work of a down-trodden or ostensibly of an oppressed population. The dedicators wrote good Greek and were evidently proud of their occupations as the ploughs, tools, and weaving combs on the inscriptions show.[54] The texts also show, however, that a new, more challenging form of Christianity would be likely to take root in the countryside, in which the Dominical imperatives would be better observed than among the established communities in the towns.

Even more important than its success among the *coloni* of the imperial estates in the Tembris valley was Montanism's spread to North Africa. The route probably lay via Rome where we know from Tertullian, *Adversus Praxean,* Montanism at one time found a favorable response from the bishop (Victor?).[55] Even before Montanus' movement had the chance to progress beyond the eastern Mediterranean countries, the new Latin Christianity in North Africa had been taking on the uncompromising character of a Montanist community. As at Lyons, persecution revealed a spirit of defiance to the authorities, nurtured by prophetic hopes and apocalyptic beliefs. On 17 July 180, the Church in North Africa enters the stage of history with a trial of confessors before the Proconsul at Carthage,[56] at a time

---

[52]W. M. Calder, *op. cit.* p. 345 and Fig. 4.

[53]E. Gibson, "The 'Christians for Christians' Inscriptions in Phrygia, Greek Text, translations and commentary," (Missoula, Montana, 1978), pp. 145-151.

[54]E. Gibson, *op. cit.*, 1, and see the illustrations reproduced in her book.

[55]Tertullian, *Adv. Praxean,* 1.

[56]Text in *The Acts of the Christian Martyrs*, ed. H. Musurillo (Oxford, 1971), pp. 86-89.

when Montanism was under pressure in its land of origin. In Carthage, however, it prospered. The New Prophecy was to leave its mark on the North African theology of the Church, its ideas of the Christian community, and its relation to society, from the beginning to the end of its existence.

Source Material

Barnard, L. W., *Justin Martyr: His Life and Thought.* Cambridge, 1967.

von Campenhausen, H., *Ecclesiastical Authority and Spiritual Power.* Edinburgh, 1969.

——————, *The Fathers of the Greek Church.* Edinburgh, 1963.

——————, *The Formation of the Christian Bible.* Edinburgh, 1972.

Daniélou, Jean, *Gospel Message and Hellenistic Culture.* Philadelphia, 1973.

Gibson, E., *The "Christians for Christians" Inscriptions of Phrygia.* Missoula, Montana, 1978.

Hanson, R. P. C., *Tradition in the Early Church.* London, 1962.

de Labriolle, P., *La Crise Montaniste*, Paris, 1913.

Lawson, J., *The Biblical Theology of St. Irenaeus.* London, 1948.

Lindars, B., *New Testament Apologetic.* London, 1961.

Ramsay, W. M., *Cities and Bishoprics in Phrygia*, 2 vols. Oxford, 1895-1897.

Schepelern, W., *Der Montanismus und die phrygischen Kulte.* Tübingen, 1929.

Shotwell, W. A., *The Biblical Exegesis of Justin Martyr.*
London, 1965.

Wingren, G., *Man and the Incarnation.* London, 1958.

Witt, R. E., *Albinus and the History of Middle Platonism.*
Cambridge, 1937.

4

Origen

There are some great figures in the Christian Church whose influence has far transcended the categories of "saint" and "sinner," or "orthodox" and "dissenter." In the west, Augustine, Francis of Assisi, Luther, Calvin and Ignatius Loyola are examples that spring immediately to mind. In the east, Origen shares with the Cappadocian Fathers and Cyril of Alexandria the role of a seminal mind whose significance has lasted from his own day to this.

He was born circa 185, the son of (probably) an Egyptian Christian or Jewish mother and a Greek father, who became a Christian, and he died at the age of 69 in 253/4. For once the dates are important. The last two decades in the second century saw, as we have mentioned, a new beginning of Christian mission, the abandonment of the hitherto prevailing sectlike existence, and the establishment, largely through Irenaeus of Lyons, of a successful orthodox defence against the Gnostic schools and Marcion. In addition, the same period witnessed the emergence of a canon of Scripture, a liturgy and rule of faith, accepted with minor variations in the main Christian communities, all of which consolidated the position of the Church and its episcopal leadership. At the other end of the period, the year 253 was a good two years after the end of the Decian persecution, and so Origen never gained his desired martyr's death, as Eusebius in his early drafts of the *Ecclesiastical History* believed he had.[1] In between, Origen's lifetime witnessed a decisive advance of orthodox Christianity and its extension throughout a great number of towns in the Mediterranean so that it threatened seriously the supremacy of the Immortal Gods of Rome as guardians of the Roman Empire, and its peoples. Origen himself contributed not a little to this reversal of fortunes. After him, Christianity was never again on the defensive, and yet, even with all his devotion to the Church and its teaching in his lifetime, his good name and orthodoxy were being challenged.

Origen was fortunate to have the historian, Eusebius of Caesarea, as an admirer. The latter's *Defence of Origen*, written with his master Pamphilus at Caesarea during the Great Persecution, has not survived,[2] but he devoted a large part of the sixth book of the *Ecclesiastical History* to a biography of his hero. Origen was, he claimed, "noteworthy from his cradle" (*H.E.* vi 2:2), a sort of infant prodigy which today we usually associate with the worlds of music or mathematics. Origen's bent was towards literature, first the classics and then the Bible. In 202-203 came a traumatic experience that revealed his convictions as a Christian. At Alexandria, as at Carthage, Rome and other parts of the Mediterranean world, there were savage outbreaks against the Christians, particularly converts. A fragment of a rescript (which I believe to be genuine) from the emperor Septimius Severus has survived, forbidding conversions to Judaism or Christianity.[3] Origen's father, Leonides, was arrested. While in prison, Origen besought him to stand firm and, it was said, was only restrained from provoking his martyrdom through his mother hiding his clothes so that

[1]See R. M. Grant, *Eusebius as Church Historian* (Oxford, 1980), p. 79.

[2]Written in six books, five of which in collaboration with Pamphilus and the sixth after his martyrdom in 310. See Grant, *op. cit.*, p. 77.

[3]Spartian, *Vita Septimii Severi*, 17:1, Script. Hist. Augustae, ed. E. Hohl (Leipzig, 1955). On the authenticity of the fragment, see Frend, "Open questions concerning the Christians and the Roman Empire in the Age of the Severi," *Journal of Theological Studies* (= *JTS*), n.s. 25:2 (1974), pp. 333-351, at pp. 342-349.

he could not go out — an insight into his true standard of value.[4] Fear of the sexual, leading to extremes of asceticism took precedence over the glory of a martyr's death.

This was soon to be proved. Among those who fled the persecution was another convert to Christianity, Clement, who for the previous decade or more had presided over the catechetical school for inquirers and converts to Christianity, administered by the bishopric of Alexandria. He had made it into a powerful force on the side of orthodoxy. Bishop Demetrius now asked Origen though only 18 to become the new leader to give regular instruction to catechumens.[5] He sold his father's library of classical and pagan philosophical works so as, in return for a modest annuity (4 obols a day) out of the proceeds, to be able to teach without fee.[5a] Then, living an ascetic life and worried at the prospect of having to instruct women as well as men, took an extreme, if not unprecedented step among Egyptian Christians[6] of accepting the literal sense of Mt 19:12 and made himself a eunuch (Eusebius, *H.E.* vi 8).

Another tendency revealed itself in these early years. His father dead, he was befriended and looked after by a wealthy lady in Alexandria. Alas for Origen, she had Gnostic sympathies and opened her house to all comers whether orthodox or Gnostic to attend services held by Paul, her Gnostic chaplain. Origen would have none of it. He would not worship with him,[7] and the deep antipathy to Gnosticism that runs through his early works may have owed something to these encounters.

Intolerant missionary zeal and extremist interpretations of Christianity would seem to be poor preparation for the man who was to become the master-theologian of his day. In his early years as a teacher at least seven of his pupils died as martyrs. Sometime in the first decade of the third century, however, a different influence began to make itself felt in his

[4]Eusebius, *H.E.*, vi:2:5.

[5]*Ibid.*, vi:3:9.   [5a]*Ibid.*, 10.

[6]For a parallel, see Justin, *I Apol.* 29 (written circa 150).

[7]Eusebius, *H.E.*, vi:2:11-14.

life. He attended lectures of the philosopher Ammonius, and became friends with Heraclas, future Bishop of Alexandria, who was already Ammonius' pupil.[8] These experiences played a decisive part in Origen's life. Latent intellectual curiosity was re-awakened, and he learnt the lessons he was to pass on to his pupil, Gregory "the Wonderworker," a quarter of a century later, that philosophy was necessary for the penetration even of Christian mysteries. He immersed himself in Plato's *Timaeus, Phaedrus*, the *Laws* and the *Letters*, and also in the Pythagorean and Middle Platonist writers nearer his own time, such as Numenius and Longinus.[9] In Heraclas, he found a trusty lieutenant, and soon he was able to hand over the elementary teaching in the school to him,[10] thus giving himself scope for working out profound and systematic study of the theological issues of the day while remaining uncompromisingly loyal to the Church.

This would take time, but the decade 210-220 saw his reputation increase. In circa 214, the governor of Arabia wrote to the prefect of Egypt and the Bishop of Alexandria asking them to send Origen to him for an interview.[11] It was the first time since Paul's discussion with the Proconsul of Cyprus, Sergius Paulus, at Paphos that a Christian teacher had been received on such a friendly official footing. He returned to Alexandria, but the next year the emperor Caracalla visited the city. He was angry that the Alexandrians had satirised him for the murder of his brother Geta (in 212). He was not amused by the apparent contamination of this Macedonian-Greek foundation by native Egyptians.[12] He ordered their forcible removal, and Origen, evidently because of his mixed Greek-Egyptian parentage, withdrew.

[8]*Ibid.*, vi:19:6, dating to circa 206-211; see T. D. Barnes, *Constantine and Eusebius* (Cambridge, Mass., 1981), p. 83.

[9]*Ibid.*, vi:19. See Barnes, *op. cit.*, pp. 86-87.

[10]*Ibid.*, vi:15.

[11]*Ibid.*, vi:19:15.

[12]*Ibid.*, vi:19:16. See, for Caracalla ordering the massacre of the Alexandrians, expulsion of Egyptians, and other reprisals against the city, Dio Cassius, LXXVIII: 22:1 and 23, and Herodian iv:9:2-3 (massacres).

He went to Palestine, made the lifelong friendship of Bishop Theoctistus of Caesarea and Alexander of Jerusalem and began to teach at Caesarea. In 216-217 he was on his travels again, this time to Rome, drawn by a curiosity to "see the ancient church of the Romans" and to hear the Christian polymath, Hippolytus.[13] He returned to Caesarea, but in 219 Bishop Demetrius peremptorily instructed him to resume his role as teacher in Alexandria.

Origen was now ready to embark on his great work of systematic theology. The *Peri Archon* (Latin: *De Principiis* — About Fundamentals) dates to circa 225, and like most of Origen's works has only survived in fragments and mainly in Latin translation (by Rufinus, circa 390), but enough remains to construct the main lines of his thought. At the outset Origen proclaimed his loyalty to the Alexandrian Rule of Faith, but claimed a right to "set down a connected series of truths agreeable to reason" in order to elucidate some statements contained in it.[14] These "footnotes" became the basis for a major treatise, against Gnostics and Marcionites in defence of orthodoxy as understood in Alexandria. Origen begins with God, who "created the world out of nothing," the God of both the Old and the New Testaments, who sent Jesus as the prophets foretold, first to preach salvation to the Jews and then the Gentiles. God, to Origen, thus combined the Platonic qualities of goodness and beauty with the active qualities of Love, Wisdom and Power. As always, Origen based himself on Scripture, in this case on Proverbs 8:22-25 (LXX) and Colossians 1:15.[15] Love, Wisdom and Power could, however, never be without their object and this was "the Word," a "kind of breath and power of God," co-eternal with Him, and intelligible to man as ever-begotten Son, and exact image of the Father (Heb 1:3).[16] The Son was therefore "a second God" revealing the Father to the divine powers and to man becoming man

[13]Eusebius, *H.E.*, vi:14:10.
[14]Origen, *De Principiis*, Preface 10, ed. P. Koetschau, *GCS* 22 (1913).
[15]*Ibid.*, 1:2:1.
[16]*Ibid.*, 1:2:5.

without ceasing to be God. Logically, however, he was less than God and the fact of his "eternal generation" differentiated him from God who had neither beginning nor end.[17] The Holy Spirit was logically superfluous to Origen's theology, for the Word itself could be held to inspire the prophets, but was found place as "the highest of angels."[18] These had been "wholly pure" for the service of God, but at some moment had become bored and rebellious, and hence had been cast out, some a greater distance, some less, from the centre of being, namely God, according to their fault.[19] Thus, the world had come into being. God "binding the souls to bodies as a punishment" and also a purifying prison. Only one soul had remained wholly pure, and that was the soul united to Christ, the Logos, which enabled him to manifest God to humanity.[20]

Origen's cosmology of graded spiritual beings resembled more that of the Gnostics than it did Genesis; Adam's fall had no place in it. Indeed, Origen insisted that the Fall of the powers was a pre-cosmic event, but it was due to their own fault. Their love towards God had cooled. They had misused their free-will. But, by the same token, they could recover their previous place in a reunited heaven. Indeed, all creation moved slowly towards the goal of ultimate restoration of divine harmony, and in this process there could be no exception. Even the Devil would one day repent and be saved, for evil was not a positive force and so could have no lasting reality.[21] Origen's sense of time was cyclical. He conceived the restoration of the Golden Age once shattered by sin but now restored through God being again all in all. Salvation was part of the process of creation. This was the

---

[17]*Ibid.*, 1:2:2, and see M. Wiles, "Eternal Generation," *JTS* n.s. 12 (1961), pp. 284-291. For the Son as "Second God," see Origen, *Dialogue with Heracleides*, ed. H. Chadwick, *Alexandrian Christianity* (London, 1954), pp. 437-455, esp. at pp. 437-438, and *Contra Celsum*, v. 39.

[18]Origen, *De Princ.* 1:3:5.

[19]*Ibid.*, 1:8:1.

[20]*Ibid.*, 2:6:3, and *Contra Celsum* v. 39.

[21]*Ibid.*, 1:6:3.

opposite to the Hebraic sense of linear time, moving from Creation to Judgement. For Origen, however, all punishment was remedial and not retributive, for in the end all souls would be purged and restored to their former heavenly state.[22]

Origen had only refuted Gnosticism by accepting some of the basic tenets of his opponents. His Trinitarian views moreover reflected those of contemporary Platonists. Plotinus' (circa 204-270) concept of the Divine existing in three separate entities is paralleled by Origen's concept of the Trinity as three distinct and graded Beings. In addition, though few, if any, Christians at the time criticised openly a theology based on the cycles of time, a great number were shocked at the mere possibility of the Devil being saved, and yet such an idea was inevitable in Origen's view of God and the universe.

Origen was more successful against the followers of Marcion. He lived in the Bible and for him every word in it was the word of God — otherwise it would not be there. The Old and New Testament could not be the work of "two Gods" as the heretics claimed, he argued. (Comment in Joh 1:13.) But he understood the Bible as Philo had before him, that is as a Platonist. Just as man and indeed creation was divided into body, soul (*psyche*) and spirit (*pneuma*) so there were three different levels of interpreting Scripture. These were the literal, the moral and the spiritual. The Christian must seek to penetrate to the heart of the meaning of each passage by the aid of intense thought and contemplation guided by the Spirit, and so understand the mysteries implicit in any word of God.[23] Thus, Origen could agree with the Marcionites that some statements in the Bible, taken literally, were nonsense. "Who is so silly," asks Origen, "to think that God like some farmer planted a paradise eastwards of Eden and set in it a visible and palpable tree of life, so that anyone who tested it with his bodily teeth would gain life." Even the

[22]*Ibid.*, 2:8:3. Compare *Contra Celsum* ii:24. See Jean Daniélou, *Origène* (Paris, 1948), p. 277.

[23]*Ibid.*, 5:2:4.

Gospels contained possible commands, such as "Salute no man by the way," or "Let the dead bury the dead."[24] The true meaning, however, was not to be revealed in the text alone. The Marcionites never troubled about spiritual meanings, yet these were there to be discovered, by comparing one text with another. Seizing on a key word or idea the exegete moved to the true message contained in a given passage. One studied the profundities of meaning contained in the Bible to become a participator of all doctrines of God's counsel.[25]

Historical data, including even place names had no serious interest to Origen. One might wonder, in that case, why it was that all the time he was writing *De Principiis*, he was attempting with enormous effort to establish an accurate text of Scripture. Again, the clue lies in Origen's passionate defence of Christianity against all opponents. Caesarea had a large Jewish community with a flourishing rabbinic school and synagogue.[26] Origen suspected that the rabbis sometimes omitted passages compromising to them, and he disliked the sheer literalism of current Jewish biblical exegesis that denied that Isaiah prophesied the Christ-Messiah on the grounds that lions did not lie down with lambs in Jesus' lifetime, nor did he ransom prisoners.[27] During his first visit to Caesarea, 215-219, he found a Jewish-Christian who taught him the elements of Hebrew. Thus equipped, he set out to establish a true text for the Old Testament so that there could be no doubts on that score, and the Jews could be refuted the better. This huge work, of which only fragments remain, was known as the *Hexapla* or six-fold edition, from the number of columns into which the texts were set out. The first column contained unvocalised Hebrew, alongside which was a Greek transliteration to

[24]*Ibid.*, 4:3:1 and 4.

[25]*Ibid.*, 4:1:14, trans. by Roberts and Donaldson, *Ante-Nicene Christian Library*, Origen I, p. 309.

[26]See C. T. Fritsch, ed., *Joint Expedition to Caesarea Maritima:* Vol. I, *Studies in the History of Caesarea Maritima.* ch. 5 (Missoula, Montana, 1975).

[27]Origen, *Letter to Africanus*, 3-5 and compare 8.

preserve the original sounds.[28] In the third column stood the Septuagint, and in the other three, versions by Aquila, a Jewish proselyte, Symmachus, an Ebionite Christian, and Theodotion, an orthodox Jewish-Christian. For the Psalms, Origen added two other versions, one which he had acquired at Nicopolis,[29] on his way to Rome, and the other "found with other Greek and Hebrew books in a jar near Jericho, during the reign of Antoninus, the son of Severus (i.e., Caracalla, 211-217),[30] a "Dead Sea Scroll" 1700 years before the discovery of the library at Qumran.

The work was not simply one of copying. For the Septuagint, Origen used symbols to point out additions and omissions compared with the other versions, so that thorough textual comparisons could be made. He also prepared a simpler *Tetrapla* containing the four Greek translations of the Old Testament[31] that survived in the library of the Church of Caesarea until Jerome's time.

Origen's exegetical work was based therefore on firm foundations, and after circa 225 he began to concentrate on this. Again, the aim was apologetic as well as scholarly. Up to this time, the one *Commentary* on John regarded as scientific was that of the Gnostic, Heracleon, written circa 170.[32] Origen determined to supersede it, and he went about the task with characteristic thoroughness. The first six words of the Gospel ("In the beginning was the Word") took up a whole volume. The surviving portion, reaching chapter 13, v. 33, covers thirty-two volumes! While in many places, as we have seen, he agreed with Heracleon[33] — the Crucified

[28]Eusebius, *H.E.*, vi:15-17.

[29]*Ibid.*, vi:16:2.

[30]*Ibid.*, vi:16:3.

[31]Origen, *Comment, in Mattheum*, xv:14, and Eusebius, *ibid.*, 16:4.

[32]See above, pp. 50-51.

[33]Thus, concerning the Pharisees' question to John the Baptist in John 1:25, Origen describes Heracleon's view that they asked their questions "out of malice" and "not wishing to learn," as "not unwise," *Comment. in Iohannem* vi:23, *GCS* 10, p. 134, and see also W. Forster, *Gnosis* i:164.

Christ was "the knowledge of babes"[34] — he was justly critical of the more fantastic allegorisations ot his predecessor.[35] His association of the spiritual and divine nature of Christ and the Eucharist anticipates Cyril of Alexandria.

In 229 he was writing the fifth book of the *Commentary* and his anti-Gnosticism was unabated. As he said:

> Today, under the pretext of Gnosis, heretics have risen against the Church of Christ. They pile on their books of commentaries. They claim to interpret the Gospel and Apostolic texts. If we are silent and do not oppose them with true teaching, famished souls will be fed with their abominations. (Comm. in Joh 5:8)

He was working at breakneck speed. He had found a patron in a rich Alexandrian named Ambrosius whom he had converted from adherence to the Valentinians, and this man provided him with materials and relays of secretaries to take down his words.[36] "The work of correction," wrote Ambrosius in a letter to a friend, referring to the *Hexapla*, "leaves us no time for supper, exercise or rest. Even at these times we are compelled to debate questions of interpolation and to emend manuscripts."[37] The scene could have been the "Scrollery" and the actors, the editors of the Dead Sea Scrolls!

A cloud, however, was rising on the horizon. Origen's relations with Demetrius had not been cordial for years. Perhaps the latter feared for the allegiance of the simpler

[34]Origen, Comment. in Iohannem 1:18, *GCS* 10, p. 23, and compare, for the value of concealing "the secret truths" of the Bible, *Contra Celsum* vi:18.

[35]For instance, Heracleon's interpretation of the whip (John 2:13-16) used by Jesus when he expelled the money-changers from the Temple, as in some way referring to Jesus' intention to construct the church "as the house of his father," as "talking rubbish," *Comment. in Iohannem* x:34 (= Forster, *op. cit.*, p. 167). See also M. F. Wiles, *The Spiritual Gospel* (Cambridge, 1960), pp. 46-47.

[36]Eusebius, *H.E.*, vi:18:1.

[37]From Ambrose's *Letter to a Friend*, ed. Lommatsch xvii, p. 5, and compare Jerome's similar account in *Ep.* 43:1 to Marcella.

members of his flock and suspected the intellectual brilliance of Origen.[38] There may, too, have been personal antipathies. Origen notes in the Prologue to the Sixth Book that he was glad to leave Egypt as a respite from the threatening storm.[39] Once more, the lure was a debate with a Gnostic champion, one Candidus, who was disturbing the churches of Achaea. He set out without Demetrius' permission in 229/230 and, taking the land-route through Palestine, allowed himself to be ordained presbyter by Bishop Alexander and Theoctistus.[40] Worse, when he finally encountered Candidus, the latter proved a wily opponent. He circulated his version of the debate and claimed that Origen had stated that the Devil could be saved.[41] In Alexandria, Demetrius' indignation knew no bounds. According to Origen, "the enemy redoubled his efforts through new writings truly alien to the Gospel and raised against us all the blasts of iniquity in Egypt."[42] Against the Gospel or no, Demetrius had a case. Origen's ordination should have been left to him. He was able to have his adversary first censured and then degraded by two successive synods where his suffragan bishops apparently outvoted the traditional rulers of the Alexandrian Church, namely the presbyters. Origen's dispute with Demetrius became a *cause celèbre*. Synods in Phoenicia, Palestine and Achaea supported Origen, but Demetrius found support in Rome — the first indication of the close alliance that was to develop between the two sees in the next two centuries. Origen either did not return to or

---

[38]For tension between the beliefs of educated and uneducated Christians in third century Alexandria, see Clement, *Stromata* vi:80:5 and 89:1, ed. O. Stählin and L. Früchtel, *GCS* 3 (Berlin, 1960). Origen himself admits (*Contra Celsum* 1:9) that the mass of Christians had little use for a philosophic understanding of their religion. For his mien with educated pagans and heretics, see Eusebius, *H.E.* vi:18.

[39]*Comment. in Iohannem*, Prologue to Bk. vi, *GCS* 10, p. 107, and compare Eusebius, *H.E.*, vi:8:4.

[40]Eusebius, *H.E.*, vi:23:4.

[41]On this incident, see H. Chadwick, *Alexandrian Christianity*, pp. 431-432.

[42]*Comment. in Iohannem* vi:Prol. 2, and see C. C. Richardson, "The Condemnation of Origen," *Church History* 6 (1937), pp. 50-64. For the case for Origen's "voluntary" withdrawal from Alexandria, see R. P. C. Hanson, "Was Origen Banished from Alexandria," *Studia Patristica* xviii (1982), pp. 904-906.

withdrew from Alexandria.[43] In 231, he settled in Caesarea
where he was to spend the rest of his life. Demetrius died in
232; his successor, Origen's friend Heraclas (232-247), did
not recall him.

There were more than twenty years of life left to him.
Once the problem of shorthand writers had been overcome
by the arrival of Ambrosius and his household in Caesarea,
he concentrated on the Bible and its exegesis. To deplore his
allegorised approach and its irrelevance today is simply to
deplore the Alexandrian tradition to which Origen was heir.
A glimpse, however, of the acuteness of his assessments
when confined to literary criticism can be gained by his
opinion regarding the *Letter to the Hebrews*. This, he says,
could not have been written by Paul, for, while the senti-
ments contained in it were "admirable and not inferior to
the acknowledged writings of the apostle," the style was far
better than that achieved by him.[44]

He showed his resilience in other ways. If he was unpopular in Egypt, he was celebrated elsewhere. Probably in 232,
he was summoned to meet the empress mother, Julia Mam-
maea, at Antioch.[45] He went and both impressed the other.
"A most religious woman," Origen's verdict on her, was high
praise indeed.[46] In March 235, however, the Severan dynasty fell. It was replaced by a rough Thracian officer called
Maximin. He made the blunt assessment that the weaknesses of the empire during the reign of Alexander Severus
(222-235) had been due to the latter surrounding himself
with Christian courtiers and advisers. These must be
removed. For the first time, persecution was threatened by
an emperor against the Christian leadership.[47] This stung
Origen into writing his *Exhortation to Martyrdom*

---

[43]Eusebius, *H.E.*, vi:26. On Ambrose's arrival in Caesarea, see Jerome, *De Vir.
Ill.*, p. 56.

[44]Eusebius, *H.E.*, vi:25:11-12.

[45]*Ibid.*, vi:21:3-4. (Date is suggested by K. Bihlmeyer, *Die "Syrischen" Kaiser zu
Rom (211-235) und die Christen* (Rothenburg, 1916), pp. 139-143.

[46]Eusebius, *H.E.*, vi:25:11-12.

[47]*Ibid.*, vi:28. See Frend, *Martyrdom and Persecution*, p. 390.

addressed to Ambrosius who had been imprisoned. Charac-
teristically, though he praises courage and endurance in the
language of philosophy, the examples of virtue that he cites
are exclusively biblical.[48]

The danger passed (236). Peace returned. Next year Origen's skills as a teacher and scholar were to be tested by an
unexpected arrival in Caesarea. The story of Gregory Thau-
maturgus ("the Wonderworker") is one of the few human
stories that have come down to us from that period. Gregory
and his brother, Athenodorus, were members of a rich Cappadocian family, and like many others of similar back-
grounds were studying Roman law in Berytus (Beirut).[49]
Their sister was married to a senior civil servant on the staff
of the governor of Palestine, whose capital was Caesarea,
and the brothers were required to form part of an official
escort to bring their sister to her bridegroom's family home
in Caesarea. Gregory had been drawn, perhaps unwillingly
toward conversion to Christianity previously, on the death
of his father when he was a boy of 14.[50] Time had passed,
however, and he and his brother seemed to be settled for an
official career in which grasp of Roman law, as well as
rhetoric would open prospects of advancement. Once
arrived in Caesarea, however, he met Origen, and this time
his adhesion to Christianity was enthusiastic and final. He
stayed in Caesarea as Origen's pupil for five years. On his
return to his home country, where he became bishop of
Neocaesarea (243-272) and a great missionary leader,[51] he

---

[48]Eusebius, *H.E.*, vi:21:3.

[49]Gregory, *Letter of Thanks to Origen*, v. 59 and 68, edited with French trans. by
Henri Crouzel, *SC* 148 (Paris, 1969).

[50]*Ibid.*, v. 49. An odd incident that must have taken place circa 215. Gregory uses
the word "Katenankgasmenos" to describe pressure put on him at the time to
become a Christian. Yet he does not appear to have been baptised, and he and his
brother were embarked on a career of public service, where even nominal adherence to Christianity could not have been an advantage. If Gregory's memory was
accurate, this is the first known instance of family pressure being exerted on an
adolescent in favour of Christianity.

[51]For Gregory's subsequent career, see Gregory of Nyssa, *Life of Gregory
Thaumaturgos*, ed. J. P. Migne, *Patrologia Graeca* (= *PG*) p. 46, cols. 893-958, and
compare Henri Crouzel, Introduction to his *Remerciement à Origène, SC*, p. 148.

sent a long letter of thanks to his master. He saw in Origen "the only man who understands divine utterances, purely and clearly, and knows how to interpret them to others."[52] Origen had in fact given him a course which led gradually forward to biblical truth. First, to use Gregory's phrase, he had prepared the ground, by clearing his pupil's soul of "weeds."[53] Then, "when he saw that these efforts were not without reward, he went back, dug over again, watered and in general used all his art and care to make us bear fruit."[54] In fact, Origen's teaching method, largely by means of long socratic-type dialogues, embraced the whole range of Greek philosophy, except for the Epicureans, and elements of physical science, leading to the study of the Bible, resulting for Gregory in self-discipline, balance and happiness. One should not attach oneself, Origen urged, to any one philosopher, however eminent, "but to God and his prophets."[55] Christianity was the highest form of philosophy, the only religion worth credence by a rational being. Its superiority over all other systems could be demonstrated triumphantly.

The reigns of Gordian III (238-244) and Philip the Arabian (244-249) saw further great advances for Christianity. Eusebius of Caesarea, writing in the next century, describes the period as one in which "the faith was increasing and our doctrine was boldly proclaimed in the ears of all."[56] So great was the harvest of souls that there were not enough reapers to garner them. Origen gives another side to this era of prosperity, describing how now office in the church was actually being sought after as a means of enhancing one's personal status.[57] His own activity continued unabated. He travelled as far afield as Athens and Nicodemia in Bithinia,[58] but most of his work seems to have been nearer home

[52]Gregory, *op. cit.*, xv:175.

[53]*Ibid.*, vii:96-97.

[54]*Ibid.*, vii:95.

[55]*Ibid.*, xv:173, and compare vi:78, 83 and 84.

[56]Eusebius, *H.E.*, vi:36.

[57]Origen, *Contra Celsum*, iii:9.

[58]Eusebius, *H.E.*, vi:32:2. For Nicomedia, see *Letter to Africanus*, 19.

and concentrated perhaps in the province of Arabia.[59]

Gnosticism was now beginning to fade. Some sects, such as the Simonians, formidable in the past, could only muster an insignificant membership.[60] Another generation would pass before the Gnostic tendency in early Christianity received a massive boost from the new Persian interpretation of Christianity proclaimed by Mani and his missionaries.[61] Meantime, Origen had turned his attention to another emergent form of Trinitarian unorthodoxy, namely Monarchianism. This concept of the relations of the Persons of the Trinity emphasised the undifferentiated unity of God (hence "Monarchianism"). "Christ," claimed Noetus of Smyrna, one of their early representatives who taught in Rome circa 200, "was the Father Himself, and the Father Himself was born, suffered and died."[62] This was a glorification of Christ, as Noetus claimed, but at the expense of rejecting the transcendence of God. At the other end of the scale, the divide between God and Christ was widened to the extent of regarding Christ as an angel, or as a perfect man on whom the Spirit had descended at baptism.[63] Both ideas could lead back to Jewish monotheism, as well as destroying the basis of the God-Logos theology expounded by Origen in the *De Principiis*.

Thus, we hear of him combatting the Monarchian views of Beryllus, Bishop of Bostra, the capital of the province of Arabia,[64] and in greater detail in the apparently unrevised text of a discussion between himself and a large group of bishops assembled to try the orthodoxy of one of their number, Heracleides. The text of the *Dialogue with Hera-*

[59]Thus, Eusebius, *H.E.*, vi:33 (re: Origen's discussions with Beryllus of Bostra) and vi:37.

[60]*Contra Celsum*, v. 11, and compare v. 62 (Carpocratian and others, practically extinct).

[61]For the spread of Manichaeism within the empire during the latter part of the third century, see P. R. L. Brown, "The Diffusion of Manichaeism in the Roman Empire," *Journal of Roman Studies* 59 (1969), pp. 92-101.

[62]According to Hippolytus, *Ad. Noetum* 1.

[63]Pseudo-Tertullian, *Against All the Heresies* 8, and Eusebius, *H.E.*, v:28:6.

[64]Eusebius, *H.E.*, vi:33.

cleides was a lucky find from a cave at Toura, south of
Cairo, where in 1941 Allied forces were digging gun positions to foil a possible Axis advance on the Egyptian capital.[65] Origen's examination of the unfortunate Heracleides
shows that Rules of Faith set out in credal terms were being
used as tests of orthodoxy, while his own methods were
unsparing and inquisitorial.

> *Origen*: I charge you, father Heracleides, God is the
> almighty, the uncreated, the supreme God who made all
> things. Do you hold this doctrine?
>
> *Heracleides*: I do. That is what I also believe.
>
> *Origen*: Christ Jesus who was in the form of God, being
> other than the God in whose form he existed, was he God
> before he came into the body, or not?
>
> *Heracleides*: He was God before.[66]

Origen pressed Heracleides to agree with him that Christ
was distinct from God, and that one could quite properly
speak of "two Gods." Heracleides became more and more
flustered as the interrogation went on. "Two Gods, but the
power is one," was his final position. Then Origen defended
what had clearly bemused his hearers by condemning both
types of Monarchianism. To "abolish the distinction
between Father and Son was virtually to abolish the Father
also." His real condemnation, however, was reserved for
those who fell into the "other blasphemous doctrine that
denies the deity of Christ,"[67] i.e., Origen's interpretation of
the biblical Christianity (Word-Man) beginning to emerge
at Antioch in rivalry to the Logos or Word-Flesh doctrines
entrenched at Alexandria. Origen's own position was far
from unassailable, for all Logos-Christology had inevitably
led to the subordination of Christ to God. This might not be

[65]See H. Chadwick, *Alexandrian Christianity*, p. 430, introduction to the *Dialogue with Heracleides*.
[66]*Dialogue with Heracleides*, p. 438.
[67]*Ibid.*, p. 439.

of great importance so long as theologians in the East were concerned with Christ's role as creator, but what would happen when Christians at the end of the century, especially the monks, sought Christ as Redeemer? Would not a subordinate being, less than God, himself need redemption?

We have now reached the year 247/48. In Rome, the year of the city's foundation was celebrated with three days and nights of jollifications, the last great bonanza untroubled by Christianity. In Caesarea, Origen produced his final classics, the *Commentary on Matthew* and the *Defence against Celsus*. Celsus' attack on Christianity had been written some seventy years before,[68] but the criticisms he had made against Christian lack of civic sense, illegal status, and vengeful and selfish monotheism were still current. "God reveals all things to us (Christians) beforehand and gives us warning (of the coming destruction of the world). He forsakes the whole universe and the course of the heavenly spheres to give attention to us alone."[69] Were such criticisms justified? Origen shows that most of Celsus' theological objections to Christianity were groundless, but less so his cultural and political charges. Christians, says Origen, were loyal to the empire blessed by the birth of the Saviour in the reign of Augustus,[70] but were not prepared to share in secular and military life as Celsus demanded that they should.[71] Their prayers and singular relation to God were sufficient service for the empire. Nothing more should be asked of them.[72]

Unfortunately, the growing perils of the times could render such attitudes suspect. In both *Contra Celsum* and the *Commentary on Matthew*, Origen foresees severe and worldwide persecution in store for the Christians.[73] In 249,

---

[68]See Henry Chadwick's introduction to his edition of Origen, *Contra Celsum*.

[69]Celsus in *Contra Celsum*, iv:23 and 28.

[70]*Ibid.*, ii:30.

[71]*Ibid.*, viii:73.

[72]*Ibid.*, viii:73; compare with viii:70 and 75.

[73]Origen, *Comment. in Matth.* 24:9 (Sermon 39) = Lommatsch iv:270.

the emperor Philip fell in circumstances not dissimilar to the revolution that had removed Alexander Severus fourteen years before. This time, however, the new emperor Decius (249-251) was a conservative-minded general, an Illyrian (Balkan) by origin, who had married into a noble Roman family. He made a supreme effort to bid for the support of the Immortal Gods and the loyalty of his subjects to drive out the invading Goths from the Roman provinces on the Danube. In January 250, prominent Christians were arrested,[74] and a general sacrifice, town by town, village by village, throughout the empire, was ordered (Spring 250). Origen himself was arrested and tortured, "his legs stretched to the fourth space in the stocks," but his refusal to sacrifice was not punished by death.[75] A few short treatises "of great use for those in need of comfort" followed.[76] His death at Tyre in 253 (or 254) indicates that he survived the Decian persecution by two years at least.

What sort of man was he? His output was fantastic, some 6,000 separate tracts and volumes,[76a] of which only a fragment have survived. But in these, there is a strong element of repetition. To have the *De Principiis* and *Contra Celsum* and *Comment. in Johann.* is to possess the essence of Origen as a theologian. He was passionately loyal to the Church though no respecter of episcopal authority.[77] With audiences he could often be hasty and impatient, and he could bore. The best and worst of Origen can be found in the *Dialogue with Heracleides*. Here we see Origen as a bully, sarcastically reducing a less well-equipped colleague to confused silence. A little later on, his audience has its revenge. A long discussion on the relation of the "interior" to the "exterior" man evidently produced yawns, for Origen is provoked into two and a half pages of abuse against the

[74]See Frend, *Martyrdom and Persecution*, p. 406.

[75]Eusebius, *H.E.*, vi:39:5.

[76]*Ibid.*   [76a] Thus, Epiphanius, *Panarion*, 64.3.

[77]Origen, *Comment. in Matth.* 16:8 and *Hom. in Num.* xii:4. For Origen as a churchman, see in particular J. Daniélou, *Origène*.

"swine" unworthy to catch his pearls of wisdom.[78] Then, at
the end of the *Dialogue*, there is Origen the idealist, the man
of strong and optimistic faith urging his hearers to "take up
eternal life. Let us take up that which depends on our
decision. God does not give it. He sets it before our face."
And a series of texts show how "the good things" of the
present life were but a shadow of the blessings of the life to
come, the "life in Christ," to which all souls were ultimately
destined.[79] Christianity, Origen foresaw, was to be the universal destiny of mankind.[80] And he believed, too, that his
explanation of God, the Trinity, the progress of man towards God, and Christianity as the religion of moral progress would guide mankind to that goal.

In much of this he was to be mistaken. There were queries
concerning his teaching in his lifetime, and he had to write
vigorously to Pope Fabian and other bishops defending it.[81]
It was not wholly due to malice that he was condemned by
Justinian's Councils of 543 and 553 and much of his writings
lost in consequence. For three generations, however, his
influence in the east was commanding. Both sides in the
Arian controversy appeal to his authority. As an ascetic, his
books inspired many an Egyptian monk. As an educationist
he showed that Greek literature and philosophy had their
due place in preparing the mind to understand the true
philosophy which was Christianity. Though he never
wavered in his faith, he proclaimed Christianity as a rational
religion, fit for independent minds, that evaded no questions however difficult or abstruse. He was a man of vision,
whose ideas prepared the way for the political theology of
Eusebius and his successors in the Byzantine Empire. He
deserved fully the title of the "greatest Christian between
Paul and Augustine."

[78] *Dialogue with Heracleides*, pp. 446-448.
[79] *Ibid.*, pp. 454-455.
[80] *Contra Celsum*, viii:69-70.
[81] Eusebius, *H.E.*, vi:36:4.

Source Material

Barnes, T. D., *Constantine and Eusebius.* Cambridge, Mass., 1982.

Chadwick, H., ed., *Alexandrian Christianity.* London, (2nd ed.) 1982.

_____, *Early Christian Thought and the Classical Tradition.* Oxford, 1966.

_____, (ed. and Eng. tr.) *Origen, "Contra Celsium."* Cambridge University Press, 1953.

Crouzel, Henri, *Bibliographie critique d'Origène.* Steenbrugge, 1971.

Daniélou, Jean, *Origen.* New York, 1955.

Hanson, R. P. C., *Allegory and Event.* London, 1954.

Nautin, Pierre, *Origène, sa vie et son Oeuvre.* Louvain, 1977.

Prestige, G. L., *Fathers and Heretics.* London, 1954,

_____, *God in Patristic Thought.* London, 1952.

Trigg, J. W., *Origen.* Atlanta, 1983.

5

Donatus and Christianity
in North Africa

So far our task has related to Greek-speaking Christianity in the first three centuries. Irenaeus, listing the areas to which Christianity had spread, makes no mention of North Africa.[1] Carthage is never referred to as an apostolic see. Its Latin-speaking Church emerges suddenly into history in 180, and it was to portray from the outset a different interpretation of the faith from its contemporaries in the eastern Mediterranean. These were concerned, as we have seen from Justin, with Christianity as a philosophy, with the mysteries of the nature of the Godhead, and the Church as the means of redeeming humanity, a universal body whose life was co-terminous with creation itself.

The North Africans, Tertullian, Cyprian, and, above all, Donatus, had a narrower view of salvation. They would be stressing the concrete reality of the Church and the Christian community. What was the Church and who were its members? Who were the saved and who were the damned? Was it a gathered community of the elect inspired by the Spirit or a universal organisation held together by the common bond of the sacraments? The world it would be associating with the Devil, and the corollary would be the

[1]See Irenaeus, *Adv. Haer.* i:10.

strictest separation between Church and state. Moreover, in the fourth century some would be seeing the Devil at work in the social institutions of the empire. The North African Church provides the first example of Christianity as a social movement intent on severing earthly fortunes in preparation for the Millennium of the saints. The confessor of the third century sometimes becomes the revolutionary of the fourth. Constantine's conversion was not universally welcomed.

In North Africa the Jewish community was represented by rabbis rather than by philosophers.[2] There was no Punic Philo. The Jews, however, were numerous and influential, and this may provide one explanation of the late emergence of a Christian community in North Africa. Christians in the early third century were sometimes regarded as schismatics from Judaism. They were called "Nazarenes" rather than "Christians,"[3] and, on the other hand, some of the terminology in use in the North African Church in the third century, such as "corban," meaning a collecting box, has a Jewish origin.[4]

The first evidence of the Christian faith provides a clue to its main features. Twelve native Christians had been arrested in a small town (Scilli) evidently near Carthage.[5] They had refused to sacrifice to the gods and had accordingly been brought before the Proconsul in his secretarium at Carthage on 17 July 180. The ensuing conversation is instructive, showing how North African Christianity was from the first a religion of protest and of opposition, in which allegiance to Christ and allegiance to the emperor were contrasted.

[2] On the Jewish community in Carthage, see M. Simon, "Le judaisme berbère dans l'Afrique chrétienne," in *Recherches d'histoire judéo-chrétienne* (Paris, 1962), pp. 30-87, and Frend, "Jews and Christians in Third Century Carthage," in *Paganisme, Judaisme, Christianisme*, Melanges M. Simon (Paris, 1978), pp. 185-194.

[3] Tertullian, *Adv. Marcionem* iv:8.

[4] Cyprian, *De Operibus et Eleemosynis* 15.

[5] For the *Acta*, see *The Acts of the Christian Martyrs*, ed. H. Musurillo (Oxford, 1977), pp. 86-89.

Saturninus the Proconsul said: "We too are a religious people, and our religion is a simple one: we swear by the genius of our lord the emperor, and we offer prayers for his health, as you ought to do, too."

Speratus said: "I do not recognise the empire of this world. Rather I serve that God whom no man has seen nor can see with these eyes. I have not stolen, and on any purchase I pay the tax, for I acknowledge my lord who is the emperor of kings and all nations."

Saturninus: "Cease to be of this persuasion."

None of the confessors complied. All admitted uncompromisingly to being Christians. They rejected a proffered delay of thirty days to reconsider their position and went cheerfully to their deaths. "Today we are martyrs in heaven. Thanks be to God." Martyrdom was to be the hall-mark of North African Christianity. The blood of martyrs was seed, Tertullian claimed in 197 (*Apologeticum* 50:16).

Twenty years later, in 202, a rather similar scene took place in Carthage. Vibia Perpetua, a *matrona* (married woman) aged twenty-two, and her slave, Felicitas, were charged before the Procurator with being Christians.[6] They admitted the accusation and defied parents (an unheard-of act) and the judge. Eventually they were executed in the amphitheatre in Carthage on 7 March 203.

It is not difficult to see in Perpetua both a strongly developed doctrine of the Spirit, the result of the inculcation of apocalyptic themes as part of her training as a catechumen, and the same element of protest as the Scillitans' stand against paganism. She believed that baptism of blood followed from baptism by water. She was also a revolutionary at heart, ready and able to defy the authorities and going to her death with sublime conviction of the rightness of her

---

[6]Ed. Murusillo, *ibid.*, pp. 103-131, and Frend, "Blandina and Perpetua: Two Early Christian Heroines," in *Les Martyrs de Lyon* (177), Colloques Internationaux du CRNS, no. 575 (Paris, 1978), pp. 167-175.

cause. She was also a Montanist,[7] accepting Montanist rituals of communion in sheep's milk and cheese,[8] and she and her companion believed passionately in the coming of the Last Days and their own ability to intercede as a "friend of the Lord" for those in torment. Binding and loosing was the prerogative of the confessor and martyr.[9] Even her life in Paradise was revealed to her and her companions in dreams, and Paradise was for martyrs alone.[10]

The rigorous religion of confession and martyrdom under the guidance of the Holy Spirit was systematised by Tertullian (circa 160-240). Donatus of Carthage (circa 280-355) was to be the direct heir of his views.

Tertullian came probably from Stoicism to Christianity, perhaps via Judaism. He applied his enormous knowledge of Roman history and literature, myth and law to the service of his new religion.[11] As he says in 197: "For who that beholds it (Christian constancy) is not stirred to inquire what indeed lies within it. Who on inquiry does not join us, and joining us does not wish to suffer, that he may purchase for himself the whole grace of God, that he may win full pardon from God by paying his own blood for it."[12]

Tertullian's religion was frankly sectarian with an emphasis on the virtues of poverty and abstinence. He regarded the Church as a sect or school, composed of convinced and dedicated individuals, the more defiant the better, mutually dependent and in their hourly expectation of the Coming scarcely concerned with the ministrations of the clergy. It

[7]See for a discussion of Perpetua's Montanism, P. de Labriolle, *La Crise montaniste* (Paris, 1913), pp. 220ff., and J. Armitage Robinson, "The Passion of St. Perpetua," *Cambridge Texts and Studies* I (1891), pp. 50-52.

[8]*Passio·Perpetuae* 4:9-10.

[9]As in the vision of Dinocrates, *Passio* 7, and for the prevalence of this view among Christians of the time, see Eusebius, *H.E.*, v:2:5 (confessors of Lyon).

[10]Tertullian, *De Anima* 55.

[11]The best general account of Tertullian is in T. D. Barnes' *Tertullian*, a historical and literary study (Oxford, 1971). Barnes' style is, however, controversial; he is severely critical of authorities ancient and modern who differ from his views.

[12]Tertullian, *Apol.* 15:16.

was congregational-based Christianity. "We are," as Tertullian said, "a society with a common religious feeling, unity of discipline and common bond of hope. We meet in gathering and congregation to approach God in prayer...." (*Apologeticum* 39:1). The Holy Spirit was on the whole congregation, the Church existing "where two or three are gathered in the unity of the Spirit." The belief in the involvement of the Spirit led:

(a) to the most rigorous moral codes which effectively cut the Christian off from his pagan fellows and inhibited any cooperation between the Church and pagan society as well as any participation in government. Tertullian's rhetorical challenge, "What is there in common between Athens and Jerusalem, the Academy and the Church" (*De Praescriptione Haereticorum* 7) and "Nothing is more foreign to us than the state" (*Apologeticum* 39) illustrate the gulf that separated the North African Christian from the rest of society in Tertullian's day. Christianity was a religion of protest.

(b) *Theologically* the emphasis on the role of the Spirit in directing the Church and its members meant that the Church in North Africa was always Trinitarian in contrast to the Binitarianism (God-Logos) of the Alexandrians. It meant also that the problems of the Church would tend to be disciplinary, centered on the nature of the Church and how its membership was to be defined.

The reception of the Holy Spirit in baptism would assume great importance in North African theology. In Tertullian's time, the African Church was already beginning to divide between the rigorists like himself and others who saw that some accommodation with pagan society was necessary and the need, too, to accept the Church as a "mixed body" on earth. In circa 220, a dispute broke out between Tertullian and Pope Callistus (217-222) on the questions of whether the Church could or could not pardon those who had committed any of the three "deadly sins," idolatry, adultery and bloodshed (derived from Judaism). In denying this right, Tertullian argued in his work *On Chastity* that Integrity was the test of Christianity and holiness the test of every Christian.[13] The Church was a community of spiritual men, not a company of bishops.[14] It was an exclusive body also, "the bride of Christ" and "dwelling of the Holy Spirit." Evil members had no place in it, and those without could not be saved.

Already in the West two opposite theologies of the Church were taking shape in Carthage and Rome respectively.

We move on a generation. Tertullian has died, and a wealthy former lawyer, Cyprian, is Bishop of Carthage. He was elected in 248, but hardly had he taken over his charge when the Church was nearly overwhelmed by the persecution initiated by the emperor Decius (249-251). Cyprian has left us with as complete an account of his ten years as bishop as anyone in the early Church, including even Athanasius. His eighty-one surviving letters and fifteen treatises are a mine of information. In addition, there are the Acts of the Seventh Council of Carthage that met on 1 September 256 to decide the controversy that once more had arisen between the churches of Carthage and Rome, this time over the nature of baptism.

Cyprian's letters show that in the generation that separated him from Tertullian many changes had taken place in the African Church:[15]

(a) Christianity had spread throughout the Roman provinces of North Africa, while remaining a predominantly urban religion.

(b) It was now entirely episcopal. Power lay in the hands of councils of bishops.

(c) Much of the evangelical fire of Tertullian's time had evaporated. It was not unusual for clergy, even bishops,

[13] *De Pudicitia*, especially pp. 18-21, ed. A. Reifferscheid, *CSEL* 20 (1890). For a discussion, see Frend, *Martyrdom and Persecution,* pp. 378-391.

[14] *De Pudicitia*, 21.

[15] For a useful summary of the advance of the Church in North Africa circa 225-250, see P. Monceaux, *Histoire littéraire de l'Afrique chrétienne*, vol. II (Paris, 1902), pp. 7-10.

to hold secular appointments (cf. Cyprian, *De Lapsis* 6).

(d) On the other hand, the underlying rigorist tradition remained, illustrated by the tradition of martyrdom maintained in certain Christian families.[16] Conversion to Christianity involved a complete rejection of one's former society and, in time of crisis, such as during the Decian persecution of 250-251, the confessors, as men of the Spirit and friends of Christ, could claim the ultimate gift of the Church, namely, that of binding and loosing on earth.[17]

Cyprian's government of the African Church was dominated by the problems raised by the Decian persecution.

First, at a council at Carthage after Easter in 251, he asserted the authority of the bishops and council over that of the confessors in the matter of re-admitting the lapsed to Communion. In making it possible for all (even those who had sacrificed) to return to the Church, he admitted tacitly the presence of ritually imperfect persons in the Church.

Second, in 254, he was confronted by an appeal by two Spanish congregations against their bishops who had lapsed during the persecution and then sought restoration from Pope Stephen. The council summoned by Cyprian decided that no delinquent cleric was tolerable as a minister in the Church. The sacraments dispensed by such a cleric were invalid and endangered the welfare of the congregation. "Nor let the people flatter themselves that they are free from contagion of the offense when in communion with a priest who is a sinner."[18]

The result was that a people "who obeyed the precepts of the Lord and fears God, ought to separate itself from a prelate who is a sinner,"[19] advice which was remembered in

---

[16]Such as that of Celerinus, Cyprian, *Ep.* 39.

[17]Thus, the confessors writing to Cyprian, in Cyprian's letters, *Ep.* 23. Cyprian they regarded as a disciplinary officer who could list deserving cases of penitent lapsed, but the act of forgiveness belonged to the confessors.

[18]*Ep.* 67:3.

[19]*Ibid.*

the crisis of the Great Persecution fifty years later.

Third, the movement inspired by the Roman rigorist, Novatian, denying re-entry into the Church to the lapsed during the persecution, had had some success in North Africa but by 255 was failing visibly. Many who had been baptised by the Novatianists now sought entry to Cyprian's Church. Were they to be baptised anew or not? Cyprian and the great majority of North African bishops thought they should be. In Rome, however, Pope Stephen, relying on the custom of his Church, believed that penance followed by laying on of hands sufficed. Was it a simple matter of ritual? The North Africans did not think so. For them baptism was the solemn moment of renunciation of the pagan world and all that it stood for. The Holy Spirit was in its waters. After emerging from the depths of the baptismal font, the Christian could count himself among those predestined to salvation.[20]

Three councils were held by Cyprian in 255 and 256 to secure agreement on the matter, and in a letter to the Mauretanian bishop Jubaianus, he made his own position clear. "We again confirmed by our sentence (of 71 bishops), ruling that there is one baptism, that appointed in the Catholic Church; and that accordingly, whosoever comes from adulterous and profane water to be cleansed and sanctified by the truth of saving water, is not re-baptised but baptised by us."[21] There was no compromise on the side of Rome, and at length, on 1 September 256, 87 bishops met at Carthage under Cyprian's presidency. In order of seniority, each man rose to give his views.[22] After an interval of more than 1700 years, these remain impressive in their simple logic and sincerity. I quote two: one from Caecilius of Bilta who spoke directly after Cyprian. "I know only one baptism in the

---

[20]See Cyprian, *Epp.* 69-75, on the issue. For scholarly discussion, see G. W. H. Lampe, *The Seal of the Spirit* (London, 1967), pp. 170-178.

[21]*Ep.* 73:1, trans. from J. Stevenson, *A New Eusebius* (London, 1959), p. 253.

[22]Text in *CSEL* 3:1, ed. W. Hartel (1871), pp. 436-461. An English translation will be found in the Ante-Nicene Library, *Cyprian*, trans. A. Roberts and J. Donaldson (Edinburgh, 1869), pp. 199-220.

church, and none out of the church. This one will be here, where there is the true hope and the certain faith. For thus it is written, 'One faith, one hope, one baptism' (Eph 4:5), not among the heretics where there is no hope, and the faith is false, where all things are carried on by lying. . . ."[23] And much else.

The second view, from one of the lesser delegates, Successus of Abbir Germaniciana: "Heretics can either do nothing, or they can do all. If they can baptise, they can also bestow the Holy Spirit. But if they cannot give the Holy Spirit, because they have not it themselves, neither can they spiritually baptise. Therefore, we judge that heretics must be baptised."[24]

An open rift between Carthage and Rome seemed inevitable. Cyprian was threatened with excommunication by Stephen, but other churches were rallying to him when the renewed onset of persecution and the death of Stephen called a halt to the quarrel.

Eventually, after a year of not uncomfortable exile, Cyprian was recalled to Carthage, tried before the Proconsul, and executed as the "ringleader of an unlawful association" on 13 September 258. His death as a martyr sanctified his views.[25]

I have told this story because it is important to realise that attitudes taken up by the opposing sides fifty years later would hardly have been possible without the tradition of the North African Church established by Cyprian. And behind Cyprian's ideas lay two generations of puritanical teaching extending back to Tertullian and beyond. Donatus was the heir to this tradition. It might even be maintained that his opponents, the Catholics, were the true schismatics.

How did schism between the two parties in the North African Church come about in 311/312? The situation arose directly out of the Great Persecution that broke out nine

[23] *Sententia* 2.

[24] *Sententia* 33.

[25] Text in *CSEL* 3:1, pp. cx-cxiv; English translation in *A New Eusebius*, pp. 260-262.

years before. Diocletian, while anxious to avoid making the Christians martyrs, was determined to uphold the predominance of the traditional guardians of the Roman people, the "immortal gods." An edict promulgated on 23 February 303 ordered the destruction of Christian churches, the cessation of all and any privileged status occupied by Christians, and the handing over of all Christian scriptures to the Roman magistrates.[26]

Though Christianity was now strong in the countryside as well as in the towns and enjoyed a considerable public sympathy, the edict was carried out to the letter. Bishops and clergy in many towns accepted the situation with various degrees of reluctance.

One or two congregations resisted, notably the Christians of Abitina in western Tunisia, who ignored the surrender of their bishop and continued to meet for prayer and praise until they were arrested and brought before the Proconsul of Africa at Carthage in February of 304. What eventually happened to them we do not know, but in prison they held a meeting at which they declared solemnly that those who communicated with a *traditor* (that is, a cleric who had handed over the Gospels to the authorities) would not share with them in the joys of Paradise. To make matters worse, they fell afoul of the Carthaginian Church authorities, and it was said later that the arch-deacon, Caecilian, actually prevented Christians' supplying them with food.[27]

The persecution ended in the spring of 305. On 1 May Diocletian and his colleague Maximian abdicated and the North African Christians gradually resumed normality. The scars remained. Congregations were divided deeply between those who were prepared to accept the ministrations of clergy who had given way, and those who were not. Matters were brought to a head on the death of the Bishop of

---

[26]Text in Lactantius, *De Mortibus Persecutorum* 12, ed. J. Moreau, *SC* 39 (Paris, 1954), and Eusebius, *H.E.*, viii:2:1 and *Martyrs of Palestine*, Preface, ed. and tr. H. J. Lawlor and H. E. L. Oulton (London, 1954).

[27]Concerning the martyrs of Abitina, see the *Acta Saturnini*, in J. P. Migne. *Patrologia Latina* (= *PL*) 8, pp. 688-715, especially paras. 18-20.

Carthage, Mensurius, in 311 (or early 312). In the ensuing election, his unpopular archdeacon, Caecilian, was consecrated bishop, and this was immediately challenged from a number of quarters.[28]

The African Church had become divided into two main parts, the communities of Carthage and other North African cities in the Proconsular province (roughly modern Tunisia), and a more rural based Christianity that prevailed in Numidia (eastern Algeria). Between 260 and 300, the senior bishop of Numidia had gained the right of consecrating each new bishop of Carthage. When, however, Secundus of Tigisis, Primate of Numidia, arrived in Carthage to perform this function, he found Caecilian already installed. There were strong rumours that one of Caecilian's consecrators had been a *traditor*, and hence his consecration was invalid. Caecilian was condemned to deposition by an ecclesiastical council,[29] and eventually, after the first appointee had died, a Numidian cleric named Donatus of Casae Nigrae ("the Black Huts") on the Sahara border was declared bishop in his stead and duly consecrated in 313.

This situation confronted Constantine on the morrow of his victory over Maxentius at the Milvian Bridge outside Rome on 28 October 312. For some reason which is not quite clear, Constantine took Caecilian's part from the outset, providing him with funds and threatening his opponents with penalities.[30] When in April 313 the latter appealed to the emperor to set up a commission of arbitration consisting of Gallic judges,[31] Constantine acted more judicially, and in his role of chief magistrate of the Roman people remitted the case to the Bishop of Rome who happened also to be an African. The hearing on 2 October 313 went against Donatus, as did the subsequent, more compre-

[28] For the African Catholic view of Caecilian and his opponents, see Qptatus of Milevis, *De Schismate Donatistarum*, I:16-21, ed. C. Ziwsa, *CSEL* 26 (1893); this was written circa 365.

[29] A fragment of this debate is preserved in the debate between a Donatist and a Catholic speaker, printed in *PL* 43, col. 774.

[30] Eusebius, *H.E.*, x:6.

[31] Augustine, *Ep.* 88:7 for this text of the petitions.

hensive disputation at the Council of Arles in August 314, while the accusation made against Felix of Apthungi that he was a *traditor* failed (February 315). Ostensibly, when the emperor finally decided against Donatus and declared Caecilian true bishop of Carthage in November of 316, the schism should have ended there and then.[32] It certainly should have done so four years later when a number of the most prominent Numidian bishops were involved in a scandal in which their respective pasts were unearthed, showing them to be worse *traditores* and criminals than by any stretch of the imagination Caecilian had been.[33] It did not. Donatus' cause, already strong, continued to flourish. Partly this was due to Donatus himself. Not much of his career is known, but the little that has survived suggests that he had great force of character. Men "swore by his white hairs,"[34] just as they might swear by the "beard of the prophet," but he combined his autocratic nature with some diplomatic ability, as he showed when he gave way to a council of colleagues on the issue of rebaptism.[35] With better luck, he might have been a western Athanasius.

Jerome rightly indicates that he nearly succeeded in rallying the whole of North Africa to himself.[36] His opponents claimed that "he claimed for himself the sovereign authority at Carthage. He exalted his heart and seemed to himself to be superior to other mortals. He wished that all, even his own allies, should be beneath him.[37] Like the Jewish highpriest, he celebrated the mysteries alone. He preferred to be known as "Donatus of Carthage."[38]

---

[32]For Constantine and the Donatists, see N. H. Baynes, *Constantine and the Christian Church*, 2nd ed., ed. H. Chadwick (Oxford, 1962), pp. 10-16, and Frend, *The Donatist Church* (Oxford, 1971), ch. 11.

[33]Recorded in *Gesta apud Zenophilum*, ed. C. Ziwsa, *CSEL* 26, pp. 189-197.

[34]Augustine, *Enarr. in Psalmum* 10:5, *PL* 36, p. 134, and Frend, *Donatist Church*, p. 154.

[35]Augustine, *Ep.* 93:43.

[36]Jerome, *De. Vir. Ill.* 93.

[37]Optatus, *De Schismate* iii:3, *CSEL* 26, p. 76.

[38]*Ibid.*

Not surprisingly, the emperor Constans refused to confirm him as sole bishop of Carthage when Donatus demanded this of him in 346, and he ended his days as an exile in Gaul.[39]

The rest of the world remained in communion with his rival Caecilian, but the movement which Donatus expressed so thoroughly continued to dominate North Africa until the beginning of the fifth century. Though suppressed by the Imperial authorities in 347 and again, more successfully, in 412, it remained a force in being until the end of the Byzantine era. Why? Donatus stood for a series of values that Cyprian and Tertullian had stood for. He represented the mainstream of North African Church development. He also attracted to his Church a revolutionary social movement. Donatism was the first expression of Christianity that combined a puritanical ethic, an episcopal organisation, apocalyptic hope and social revolutionary aspirations.

(a) His doctrine of the Church put integrity first. Caecilian's consecration was invalid and hence sacraments dispensed by him and his followers were invalid. The Church was a small body of the Elect. Its progress had been described in the Parable of the Tares.[40] True Christians had to separate themselves from the false. It was no concern of theirs if the rest of the world associated with Caecilian. They would suffer his fate.

(b) He insisted on the complete separation of this Spirit-directed Church from the state. His attitude is summed up by his question to the commissioners sent by the emperor Constans to North Africa in 347, "What was the emperor to do with the Church?"[41] In this he said in fewer words, and more bluntly than others, what most western Christians thought.[42]

---

[39] Jerome, *loc. cit.*

[40] See Augustine, *Contra Epistolam Parmeniani* ii:2:5, *PL* 43, 52.

[41] Optatus, *De Schismate*, iii:4, *CSEL* 26, p. 73.

[42] For instance, Hosius and Hilary of Poitiers. See S. L. Greenslade, *Church and State from Constantine to Theodosius* (London, 1934), pp. 44-45.

(c) He represented the traditional African interpretation of Christianity in which penance, suffering and martyrdom played a predominant part in an age when the empire was officially Christian. Not surprisingly, some fifty years after his death, he was still looked back to as "the man who reformed the Church in Africa."[43] Another factor makes his period as bishop of Carthage remarkable. By this time Christianity had become overwhelmingly the religion of North Africa, paganism being represented mainly among the old governing class in the towns. The conversion of the countryside, especially the inhabitants of the imperial and private estates of Numidia and Mauretania had strange results. Chapels sprang up in Numidian villages in a manner reminiscent of Methodist and Baptist chapels in Wales and northern England in the nineteenth century.[44] Some of the peasants were no doubt contented with the not unrewarding agricultural round, punctuated with rowdily festive celebrations of the anniversaries of martyrs whose relics were housed in the chapel of their village.[45] The fragments of glass drinking vessels found in quantity on some of these sites says much for the character of the celebrations.[46] Hymns of praise sung with full-throated roar, punctuated by biblical readings (in Latin, so far as can be judged) and a Eucharist that included commemoration of the martyr and feasting in an *agape* were features of their services.[47] Their inscriptions were summed up by an inscription from Thamalluta in eastern Mauretania, "Praise ye the Lord and rejoice, ye righteous, let us glory in the Lord with a true

[43]Augustine, *Contra Cresconium*, ii:56:62.

[44]See A. Berthier and colleagues, *Le Christianisme antique dans la Numidie centrale* (Algiers, 1942), Map.

[45]For a description of a parallel Catholic celebration of the anniversary of the martyr Leontius at Hippo in circa 393, see Augustine, *Epp* 22 and 29.

[46]See art. "Morsott" in *Dictionnaire d'archéologie et de liturgie*, and also "Agape," *ibid.*, 1:1, col. 830.

[47]See P. Monceaux, *Histoire littéraire*, iv. pp. 149-151.

heart." "Praise to God" (*laus Deo* or *Deo laudes*) was the Donatist watchword.[48]

It also became the watchword of some of whom Donatus and his colleagues did not approve, at least at the outset. Just as Luther's Reformation inspired insurrectionary hopes among the German peasants, so Donatus' reform of the North African Church on traditional lines, and his rejection of the claims of Caecilian and of a Christianity acceptable to the emperor and his officials, seems to have set off a similar movement among the peasants of Numidia and eastern Mauretania. By 340 the Donatists had become associated with rising social revolutionary aspirations among the peasants. In many respects the North African Circumcellions resembled the Egyptian monks, even to their monastic-type clothing.[49] Both movements had a background of protest against extortionate taxes, moneylenders, and rich and powerful landlords. Both saw themselves as heirs to the martyrs. The monks, however, settled down as loyal subjects of the empire. The Circumcellions did not. They felt themselves still to be "athletes" (*agonistici*) and they formed an identifiable group under their "captains of the saints" opposed to the established order in the countryside and determined to reverse the roles of slave and master. "No one," said Optatus of Milevis, "could feel sure of his estates. In those days no creditor possessed the liberty of exacting payment of a debt." Masters and slaves suddenly found their positions changed round. Rich men driving comfortable vehicles would find themselves pitched out and made to run behind, while their slaves took over.[50] Behind this was the Circumcellions' belief that the Devil, once a persecutor, could now be identified with the great of this world. Death in challenging the social

---

[48]*Ibid.*, iv, p. 455, and compare Augustine, *Contra Litteras Petiliani* ii:65:146.

[49]See my "Circumcellions and Monks," *JTS* n.s. 20 (1969), pp. 542-549 (bibliography of earlier works).

[50]Optatus, *De Schismate* iii:4.

order would be martyrdom and the means of gaining Paradise. Suicide by jumping over a cliff was an acceptable substitute.[51] No wonder when, in 347 Constans' emissaries arrived in North Africa to inquire about the state of Donatus' Church and were met by Circumcellions, the authorities reacted sharply. The Circumcellions were dispersed, Donatus exiled, and Donatist churches handed over to the Catholics.

In the second half of Constantius II's reign, the Donatist Church should have ceased to exist. Unity was proclaimed under the aegis of the Catholic bishop of Carthage, Gratus. Donatus himself and his leading colleagues were exiled to Gaul and for fourteen years the Catholics were the undisturbed representatives of the North African Church. Around the year 348, Gratus held a council designed to consolidate the newly achieved victory,[52] and although Donatist influence was still powerful (as the plaint of the Bishop of Madaura showed, the people regarded his rival as "father" while he was relegated to the position of "father-in-law"![53]), it might have become a wasting asset. As it was, some towns in northern Numidia, such as Augustine's home, Thagaste, were won over permanently to Catholicism.

Constantius II, however, died on 3 November 361, and early the next year, in a deliberate move to exacerbate sectional differences among Christians, his successor, Julian "the Apostate," allowed all those exiled under his predecessor to return home. The Donatist leaders had evidently petitioned the emperor,[54] even before the latter's decision

---

[51] For Circumcellion suicides in this manner, see Augustine, *Contra Gaudentium* 1:28:32 and L. Leschi, "Apropos des epitaphes chrétiennes du Djebel et Nifen-Nisr," *Revue Africaine* 82 (1940), pp. 35-40. For the appearance of this phenomenon as early as Gratus' Council, see Canon 2 in *Corpus Christianorum series latina* (= *CCSL*) 149, ed. C. Munier (Turnhout, 1974), p. 4.

[52] Munier, *CCSL* 149, pp. 3-10.

[53] Canon 12.

[54] Augustine quotes part of the letter written by leading Donatists in exile to Julian in *Contra Litteras Petiliani* ii:97:224, and compare *Ep.* 93:4:12.

taken in February 362, and back they came bent on vengeance.[55] In a few short weeks, the Catholic ascendancy was
a thing of the past, and the Donatists were as firmly established in North Africa as they had been before the fateful
mission of Paul and Macarius.[56]

Before he died, Donatus had found a successor. He was
not an African but "a Gaul or Spaniard" in Optatus of
Milevis' calculatingly vague expression.[57] He was to lead the
Donatist movement until his death in 391/392 and, in Au-
gustine's view, "consolidated Donatism,"[58] His name was
Parmenian.

In Parmenian's long rule, Donatism moved from being a
protest against Caecilian and his followers to something like
the established Church in North Africa with a characteristic
theology. For this, Parmenian himself was partly responsible. His theology of the Church may sound crude, but it
fitted the exclusive outlook of the disciples of Cyprian. He
accepted that the Church was "the Bride of Christ." Every
bride, however, possessed endowments. The question at
issue was which of the two rival churches in North Africa
had better claim to these "endowments." In Parmenian's
view the Donatists succeeded. They could claim "the
cathedra" (episcopal seat representing unity and authority),
the *angelus* or angel hovering over the waters of baptism,
the *fons* or baptismal font, the *sigillum* or seal of baptism,
and the altar.[59] To the Catholics could be applied the text
from Psalm 141:5: "Let not the oil of the sinner anoint my
head."[60] They had fallen irredeemably through their adherence to Caecilian.

It is interesting to see how someone uninvolved in the

[55]The scenes are graphically described by Optatus in Bk. II of *De Schismate*
(ii:16-17) and compare vi:3.

[56]See Frend, *The Donatist Church*, ch. xiii (the Age of Parmenian).

[57]Optatus, *op. cit.*, ii:7. For a sketch of Parmenian, see P. Monceaux, *Hist.
litteraire* v., pp. 220ff.

[58]Augustine, *Sermo* 46:8:17.

[59]Optatus, *De Schismate* ii:6. An alternate concept could be the "angel of the
church" as in Rev. 2-3.

[60]*Ibid.*, iv:7.

initial controversy could so readily accept the Donatist standpoint. The Donatists were not the only champions of the "gathered Church" in the West. Parmenian had read some of Cyprian's theology and had accepted it readily. Hilary of Poitiers was also to be found in Donatist libraries.[61] We also discern aspects of baptismal ecclesiology prevalent in some parts of the West with the ideas of "the angel" hovering over the baptismal waters (not "the spirit" as in North African tradition), and the terminology of *fons* and *sigillum* applied to baptism. Parmenian, in addition, accepted Cyprian's insistence on right faith as a condition of valid baptism and Donatus' theory of Church-State relations.[62] Interesting, too, that his Catholic opponent, Optatus of Milevis, could make little headway with his arguments that the Church must be universal and in communion with Rome, that the empire protected the Church and was owed loyalty, and, in addition, Donatism had no valid historical justification.[63]

The second theologian of the era of Parmenian was a far greater thinker than his superior in the Church. Tyconius (fl. 375-385) was a Donatist layman of Proconsular Africa,[64] and reflects the absorbing interest in theological problems characteristic of some of the Donatist laity in the last quarter of the fourth century. Tyconius was a Donatist. He hated "the false Church" of the Catholics, and, while dismissing the Circumcellions as "superstitious brethren," was convinced that the Church of Donatus represented the true Church in Africa.[65]

His interest, however, lay in Scriptural exegesis, and the "Rules" that he set out for interpreting the text of the Bible were still acceptable among Western exegetes in the Early

[61]As in that of Vincentius of Cartenna, see Augustine, *Ep.* 93:9:31.

[62]Thus, Optatus, *De Schismate* i:22.

[63]*Ibid.*, ii:3.

[64]For literature on Tyconius, see Berthold Altaner and Alfred Stuiber, *Patrologie*, 7th ed. (Freiburg, 1966), p. 373.

[65]Tyconius, cited from T. Hahn, *Tyconius-Studien* (Leipzig, 1900), p. 68.

Middle Ages.[66] Typological interpretation based on close attention to the text, however, revealed problems that he could not solve on the basis that the Church was represented only by the Donatists. What about texts relating to the "wheat *and* tares," the bride who was "black *and* comely"? Surely on earth the Church must be a mixed body, and there must be some genuine Christians beyond the shores of Africa?[67] Tyconius was seeing human society divided into conflicting Cities, but membership in these Cities was determined not by ecclesiastical allegiance but by the direction of the individual will. In the past, these had been characterized by Abel, the patriarchs, prophets, disciples of Christ, and the followers of Donatus, contrasted with Cain, Herod, Judas, and Caecilian. These were ever in conflict, the righteous suffering and wicked persecuting, but in essence they were spiritual contests, embracing Christians the world over, not restricted to the narrow stage of North Africa.[68] It was this last notion that Parmenian could not accept. The "Two Cities" were becoming a norm in Donatist interpretation of history. Twenty years later in 401, Petilian, Donatist Bishop of Constantine, was to make great play with this chain of personalities and events in denouncing the "kings of this world" and justifying Donatist ideas of the relationship between Church and empire;[69] but no Donatist leader could concede that *de facto* true Christians existed outside North Africa. Tyconius could not agree and reluctantly Parmenian excommunicated him (circa 385).[70]

Tyconius influenced Augustine's thought as the latter generously admitted,[71] and we must consider, finally, Augustine's answers to Donatist theology. Augustine (354-430) had been brought up in Thagaste, one of the few towns that

---

[66]For instance, Bede. See F. C. Burkitt, "The Book of Rules of Tyconius," *Cambridge Texts and Studies* iii, 1 (Cambridge, 1904).

[67]See Frend, *Donatist Church*, pp. 203-204.

[68]*Ibid.*, p. 204, and pp. 316-318.

[69]Augustine, *Contra Litteras Petiliani* ii:92:202.

[70]Augustine, *Contra Epis. Parmeniani*, i:1:1.

[71]*Ep.* 41:2.

had remained true to the Catholic allegiance after the restoration of Donatism under Julian.[72] While he had Donatist relatives,[73] he does not seem to have come into serious contact with Donatism until some time after his return to North Africa from Italy in 388, perhaps as late as 390.[74] Down, however, until 398, the Donatists, despite an embarrassing split in their own ranks, the Maximianist schism, remained in the ascendant. Imperial officials in North Africa were prepared to accept the Church led by Parmenian's successor, Primian, as at least an official "Catholic" body.[75] This situation changed in 398 when at least one powerful Donatist leader supported the rebel, Count Gildo, in his rebellion against the authority of the Emperor Honorius in Italy.[76] The rebellion failed and, whether they were guilty or not, the Catholics could now dub their opponents "Gildoniani." Moreover, thanks to the imaginative and skillful organisation carried out by the Catholic bishop of Carthage, Aurelius (391-426), the Catholics were able to take advantage of the situation. In Augustine, now Bishop of Hippo, a considerable town on the Numidian coast, they had a writer and controversialist who would exploit it to the full.

Augustine's aim was to force the Donatists into a conference to decide "Which was the Catholic Church in Africa," they or their opponents. He was confident that his theological arguments, backed by the historical weakness of the Donatist case, would carry the day. In the background always was his readiness to involve the aid of the state to enforce its anti-heretical legislation against the Donatists.[77]

[72]*Ep.* 93:5:14.

[73]Such as his cousin Severus; see *Ep.* 52.

[74]Probably until he was appointed presbyter and found himself involved with a divided Christian community. See Possidius, *Vita Augustini* 6 and 7.

[75]Frend, *Donatist Church*, p. 219.

[76]Optatus of Thamugadi: for the view that he did not receive widespread support, see E. Tengström, *Donatisten und Katholiken*, pp. 84-90.

[77]E.g., Augustine, *Contra Epistolam Parmeniani* i:10:16, and see Frend, *op. cit.*, p. 241, and P. R. L. Brown, "Ausgustine's Attitude toward Religious Coercion," *JRS* 54 (1964), pp. 109-116.

By 397 he had already decided in his own mind that Donatus was a "heretic" and not merely a "schismatic."[78] In the next fourteen years he used all his gifts as a debater and negotiator to achieve his ends. In quick succession he wrote the three books *Against the Letter of Parmenian*, another three *Against the Letter of Petilian*, seven books *On Baptism against the Donatists*, arguing on thin ice against the conclusions of Cyprian's council of September of 256, though extolling the virtues of Cyprian himself. All this was in the years 399-402. Next year he issued a challenge through the authorities to the Donatists to debate their cause in open conference with the Catholics. This was refused, but two years later, largely due to Augustine's initiative, the Donatists were formally proscribed by Imperial decree (February-March 405).[79] However, these laws were not very effective. The Donatists lost some support in the Romanized cities, and some previously friendly landowners switched sides,[79a] but the great mass of Donatists remained faithful to their Church. Not till May of 411 was Augustine able to bring his opponents to conference at Carthage and, after three days of debate in which he himself took a decisive part, to have them formally condemned (January 30, 412).[80] This time the measures were more successful. It may well be that for a few years landowners who had previously been reluctant to act against their Donatist peasantry now concluded that their interest was to support the authorities[81] and the belated alliance between the two forced the Donatists on to the defensive, despite renewed depredations by the Circumcellions. Such was the situation when the Vandals landed in North Africa in the spring of 429.

[78]Thus, the title, "Contra Epistolam Donati heretici," of Augustine's (last) book against Donatus, *Retract* 1.21.

[79]*Cod. Theod.* xvi:5:37 and 39 (February-December 405).

[79a]See S. Lancel. *Actes de la Conference de Carthage* i, *SC* 195 (Paris, 1972), pp. 119-130, on the Donatist losses after 400.

[80]*Cod. Theod.* xvi:5:52.

[81]For instance, Celer, a big landowner in the Hippo diocese: Donatist to circa 405 and thereafter Catholic.

What arguments did Augustine deploy against his opponents? First, the Donatist doctrine, especially their understanding of the nature of the Church, was at fault.[82] The Church by definition must be universal for how else could God's promises to Abraham — "I will give thee the heathen for an inheritance," and "In thy name shall all nations be blest" — be fulfilled if that were not so? To this end, the Church in Africa must at least be in communion with the apostolic sees.[83] (Augustine, unlike Optatus of Milevis, laid no great stress on the special position of the Roman see.) Thus, the Church on earth must be a "mixed body," the definition of its true members deferred to the Last Day, not carried out recklessly in the "time of Donatus."[84] It followed that the holiness that the Donatists claimed for themselves was also a characteristic of that Day only and that their claim that they alone could dispense a valid baptism was spurious. Sacraments originated in Christ, the Head of the Church. The minister was simply the channel of grace, and if he gave the sacraments in the name of the Trinity, they were valid, whatever his personal state might be. Schism — "lack of charity" — was the worst of sins, and sacraments dispensed by a Donatist schismatic, though valid, were not "efficacious."[85] Here Augustine for once lapsed into casuistry, for if baptism in the name of Christ was valid through His power, it could hardly lack efficaciousness! Finally, the Donatists had no historical case against Caecilian. The latter and his consecrators had been cleared of all charges. Their schism was without justification.

How were peace and unity to be restored? Argument alone did not suffice. Donatists would listen with various degrees of impoliteness and remain Donatists. Augustine, for all his occasional parade of African patriotism,[86] was

[82]See G. G. Willis, *Saint Augustine and the Donatist Controversy* (London, 1950), ch. iv.

[83]See Augustine, *Ep.* 53:1.

[84]*Contra Epist. Parm.* i:14:21.

[85]Augustine, *De Baptismo contra Donatistas*, iv:9:13.

[86]*Ep.* 17 to Maximus the Grammarian (circa 389-390).

and remained a Roman provincial. Hippo was a "Roman city" whose magistrates should enforce "Roman laws" against heretics.[87] When the chance was offered in 399, Augustine was quick to point out in his reply to "the letter of Parmenian" that if the emperor could punish prisoners and other criminals, he could also punish heretics.[88] Not every persecution was unjust, he told Petilian.[89] It is true that Augustine may have envisaged persecution as something like "fatherly correction," inconveniences imposed in the interests of paternal discipline. Unfortunately, there was never a possibility that it would turn out that way: imperial officials carrying out their master's instructions were not known to be gentle in their methods,[90] and this Augustine knew himself. His espousal, therefore, of the use of force against the Donatists, justified by his reading of Luke 17:23 ("Compel them to come in") was carefully calculated. It was, as he told a Donatist priest of Mutugenna in his own diocese, better to be punished on earth than to suffer everlasting damnation.[91] We cannot, therefore, acquit Augustine of his share in justifying the persecution of heretics and unbelievers, though we may sympathize with the problems of a Catholic bishop confronted by a countryside dominated by the Circumcellions often led by Donatist clergy.

The Donatists represented the "gathered Church" with all its assets — holiness, integrity, separation from the world, acceptance of the Judgment and the Lord's coming in a community permanently under the guidance of the Spirit. But it also carried its disadvantages — narrowness of vision, self-righteousness, and harsh fanaticism against opponents. Augustine's idea of the Church was perhaps more realistic in the age of Theodosius and his ideas of Church-state relations more practical. Kings, even Nebuchadnezzar, could

[87] *Ep.* 34.

[88] *Contra Epist. Parm.* i:10:16.

[89] *Contra Litt. Petil.* ii:85:189, and compare *Ep.* 93:5:16-18.

[90] Thus, Augustine, *Epp.* 103 and 104.

[91] *Ep.* 173, and compare *Ep.* 93:6:20.

repent and be schooled into serving the Church with laws that favoured its expansion and protected it against enemies.[92] Compromise and expediency are not, however, always the most acceptable positions in religious life. As we shall see, the Council of Chalcedon of 451 was to provoke the massive popular reaction of the Monophysite movement.

Source Material

Brisson, J. B., *Autononomisme et Christianism e dans l'Afrique romaine*. Paris, 1958.

Brown, Peter, *Religion and Society in the Age of St. Augustine*. London, 1972.

Frend, W. H. C., *The Donatist Church*, 2nd ed., Oxford, 1971.

—————, *Martyrdom and Persecution in the Early Church*. Oxford, 1965.

Greenslade, S. L., *Schism in the Early Church*. London, 1952.

Hinchliff, P., *Cyprian of Carthage*. London, 1974.

Markus, R. A., *Saeculum: History and Society in the Theology of St. Augustine*. Cambridge, 1970.

Tengström, E., *Donatisten und Katholiken*. Göteborg, 1964.

Willis, G. G., *Saint Augustine and the Donatist Controversy*. London, 1950.

---

[92]*Contra Litt. Petil.* ii:92:212.

6

Pelagius

In the controversies surrounding Pelagius and his views on grace and baptism, we move back to intellectual debate. Donatism in the time of Augustine was as much a social as a religious movement. The martyr ideal, the imitation of the Maccabees, and the belief in the exclusive integrity of the Church combined to attract to Donatism those who wished to see profound changes in the social as well as the religious structure of Roman Africa. Pelagianism had its social aspects, and those who espoused it were often zealous for social reform, but it was primarily a movement within fairly narrow social confines, first in Rome, then with the intervention of Augustine in 411 among Christian intellectuals in Rome and Africa, and thence spreading to Constantinople where it damaged fatally Nestorius' credit with the Roman Church. Its expansion to Britain at about the same time remains a mystery, and similarly what part if any it played in the revolutions that ended Britain's connection with the empire in and after 410.[1]

Pelagius may or may not have been a Briton by birth. He was not a monk. We find him in Rome in the 380s as the

---

[1] See the ingenious article by J. N. L. Myres, "Pelagius and the End of Roman Britain," *Journal of Roman Studies* 50 (1960), pp. 21-36, but also for a contrary viewpoint, W. Liebschutz, "Did the Pelagian Movement Have Social Aims?" *Historia* 12 (1963), pp. 227-241.

spiritual advisor of the most important of the Christian Roman families, namely the Anicii.[2]

Between 350 and 380 Christianity had gained ground steadily among the traditionally pagan upper classes. There had been some striking conversions, such as that of the Neo-Platonist philosopher Marius Victor (circa 360) described in Augustine's *Confessions* (Bk. 8), and many of the women in the senatorial households were enthusiastic Christians,[3] but on the whole, the menfolk continued to be loyal to the national religion.[4] Christianity was still a minority religion in the Senate at the time of the Altar of Victory controversy, 382-384, when the pagan senators, led by Quintus Aurelius Symmachus, pleaded in vain at the court of Valentinian II for the restoration of the altar and statue of Victory to the Senate House whence the emperor Gratian (367-383) had had it removed.[5] In a few years, however, the situation had changed drastically. First in 388 and then in 394 the emperor Theodosius I (379-395) had overthrown successive usurpers who had tried to seize power in the western provinces of the empire. His resulting prestige and ceremonial visit to Rome sufficed to bring about a massive swing among the senators toward Christianity, which thenceforth became the predominant religion in the city.

The tone of the new senatorial Christianity in the early years of the fifth century remained strongly patriotic. The Spaniard, Prudentius, counsellor to Theodosius' son and successor Honorius (395-423) reflects this outlook. In writing a poem, ostensibly directed against Symmachus (*Contra Symmachum*) he recalled Rome's past with pride and looked forward to her greater future as the Christian capital

[2]Augustine, *Letter* 186:1, knew him as a "Brittonem." For his connections with the Anicii, see G. de Plinval, *Pélage: ses écrits, sa vie, et sa réforme* (Lausanne), 1943), pp. 214-216.

[3]See P. R. L. Brown, "Aspects of the Christianization of the Roman Aristocracy, *JRS* 51 (1961), pp. 1-11.

[4]For instance, see Jerome, *Letter* 107:1, and Brown, *loc. cit.*

[5]Symmachus, *Relatio* iii, English translation in *Prefect and Emperor: the Relations of Symmachus, A.D. 384*, ed. R. H. Barrow (Oxford, 1973), and Ambrose, *Letter* 17 and 18.

of the world.[6] Roman society was by no means pessimistic about the future of the Roman world, even within a decade of the fall of Rome to Alaric the Visigoth. In this new Christianised Roman society, Pelagius and his followers were assured a hearing.

The big Christian households now had their spiritual advisors in the same way that their forebears had found a place for philosophers as tutors for their children. In 382 Pelagius seems to have been one such, while Jerome was spiritual advisor to another aristocratic house, the Aemilii. This included the talented women Paula and her two daughters Eustochium and Blesilla. They formed a pious group, the women studying their Bibles in Hebrew and observing a strict and uncompromising asceticism in their palace.[7]

Asceticism, however, though a popular movement in the East, was disliked in the West. It was connected with the sect of the Manichees who were ascetic dualists sharing many of the attitudes of the Gnostics and were suspected of practising obscene parodies of Christian rites.[8] Jerome knew the risks but did not heed them. Moreover, he was arrogant and unsympathetic toward pagan society. "Learn from me a holy arrogance. You are different from them," he tells Eustochium (*Letter* 22:16). In October 384, Blesilla died as the result of her spiritual exertions. In a few months Jerome had been hounded out of Rome, never to return.[9]

Christian piety among the Roman aristocracy took a different tack for the next twenty years. This was where Pelagius was important. He was to be active in Rome for "a very long time," perhaps as much as thirty years, if he had met and fallen afoul of Jerome there.[10] He was only forced

[6]Prudentius, *Against Symmachus*, 1:461-469 and 585-590.

[7]Jerome, *Letter* 108:26.

[8]Jerome, *Letter* 22:38 (Manichaean "nuns" in Rome) and Augustine, *Letter* 31:4 to Paulinus of Nola. See, for their reputation among the orthodox for obscene rites, Pope Leo, *Letter* 8. The bread which Augustine sent to Paulinus was later suspected of being some Manichaean sacramental concoction!

[9]Jerome, *Letter* 45. See J. N. D. Kelly, *Jerome*, p. 114.

[10]Pelagius complained that Jerome "hated him as a rival;" quoted by Augustine *Contra Julianum* ii:36, and for his long stay in Rome, *Ep.* 177.

to leave the city on its fall to Alaric on 24 August 410. Personally, he does not seem to have been very forceful. His influence lay in his powerful logic and well-argued optimism in an era when growing fear of the approaching Judgment induced among many aristocratic Christians of Rome and their imitators in the West a view that complete acceptance of Christianity involved rejection of secular interests and duties, as well as personal asceticism.[11] Pelagius was of a different world. Asceticism and moralism may have been characteristics of his teaching, but they were united with activities that were not those of the aristocratic Western monk. During his time at Rome he wrote his *Commentaries* on the Pauline epistles in which he used *inter alia* Augustine's anti-Manichean works, Hilarius (Ambrosiaster), Ambrose, and Rufinus of Aquileia's translations of Origen's writings. On this platform of respectability and orthodoxy (or near-orthodoxy) he had, if one may follow Torgny Bohlin, evolved many of the ideas that were later to be denounced as "Pelagian."[12] His aim had been to challenge the theology of the Arians and Manichees, the one for their denial of the true Godhead (and also the true humanity) of Christ, and the latter for their emphatic denial of his humanity.

The Manichees were the more actual challenge, for their activity in Rome during the 380s is attested by Augustine as well as by Jerome.[13] Two of the main Pelagian tenets, the sovereignty of man's free will and the duty of the Christian to reform the lot of his contemporaries (not least by rejecting wealth as a standard of value) can be seen as a challenge to the Manichees. The latter were determinist and dualistic in theology and rejected any sort of productive work, let alone reforming zeal such as Pelagius sought to instill in his followers.[14]

[11]See Peter Brown's article, "Pelagius and His Supporters," *JTS* n.s. 19 (1968), pp. 93-114 = pp. 183-207 of *Religion and Society in the Age of Saint Augustine.*

[12]Torgny Bohlin, *Die Theologie des Pelagius und ihre Genesis* (Uppsala, 1957), pp. 10-15.

[13]Augustine, *On the Morals of the Manichees*, xx:74-75.

[14]Bohlin, *op. cit.*, p. 15.

Pelagius had made human free-will the basis of his system. This was God's gift to mankind and it implied an ability to avoid sin. Grace could be defined as this capacity, reinforced by the grace of revelation given by the Law and the Prophets and by Christ, and by the remission of sins.[15] Hence, of human nature, Pelagius said, "we classify these faculties thus, arranging them into a certain graduated order. We put in the first place *posse*, power, in the second, *velle*, will, and in the third *esse*, realisation. The power we place in our nature, the volition in our will, and the realization in accomplishment. The first of these faculties expressed in the term *posse* is especially assigned to God, who has bestowed it on his creature. The other two, indicated in the terms *velle* and *esse* must be referred to the human agent because they flow forth from the fountain of his will."[16]

Man could therefore theoretically live without sin, but what if he failed to do so? Pelagius, as against the Manichees and later Augustine saw sin as external to man, the product of the human will, but to choose sin and not righteousness involved the loss of free will. Hence, revelation itself needed to be reinforced by the effect of Christ's death and resurrection into which the believer was baptised.[17]

Pelagius laid great stress on the purpose and effect of baptism. In this he resembles the Donatists as he does in his insistence on holiness as the aim of the individual and the group. But he does not institutionalise this notion and associate it with the Church. Individuals are to be holy, "authentic Christians," as he would say. Such Christians would form part of a dedicated group. "God wanted His people to be holy. Blessed is the people who form part of

[15]As made clear by Pelagius defending his views at the Council of Diospolis in 415. See R. F. Evans, *Pelagius: Inquiries and Reappraisals* (London, 1968), pp. 106-113.

[16]Pelagius, cited by Augustine, *De Gratia Christi* 5, translated by J. Stevenson, *Creeds, Councils, and Controversies*, p. 217.

[17]Christ was example, revealing to men what their true nature was capable of by continually putting to death sinful desire. The paradox of his teaching revealed to mankind how it should behave in concrete instances. See Evans, *op. cit.*, p. 107.

God's people whom He has chosen to be His heirs,"[18]

The baptised Christian had acquired the means to live a life of conformity with God's law. As one wrote, "When I lived at home, I thought I was being a worshipper of God .... Now, for the first time, I have begun to know how I can become a true Christian."[19]

The key lies in the last sentence. The baptised Christian was responsible for his own future. He could accept or reject the ideal of perfection. He would be rewarded or condemned accordingly.

On the practical side, the Pelagian was a social reformer — in this he would contrast with the follower of the Western ascetics Jerome and Paulinus of Nola and with Augustine himself. Three quotations of a Pelagian Briton(?) living in Sicily:[20]

(a) "One man owns a large mansion with costly marbles, another has not so much as a small hut to keep out the cold and heat. One man has vast territories, another has a little bit of turf to sit on and call his own...." Did God will universal inequality? the writer asks. "Does the poor man feel the sun less keenly than the rich? Should there be one law for the poor and one for the rich?"[21]

(b) The same, "When does your prosperous man remember the frailty of his condition? Listen to the rich man calling the beggar "wretch," "beggar," "rabble," because he dares to open his mouth in "our" presence."[22]

(c) Magistrates were described as "having under their very eyes, the bodies of men like you in nature" beaten with whips of lead, broken with clubs, burnt in the flames.[23]

---

[18] Pelagius, *De Vita Christiana* 9 (*PL* 40, 1038).

[19] *Epistola Honorificentiae tuae* 1; cited from P. R. L. Brown, *Augustine of Hippo*, p. 347.

[20] For this individual, see J. Morris, "Pelagian Literature," *JTS* n.s. 16 (1965), pp. 27-60, especially pp. 37-59.

[21] *De Divitiis* 8:2; cited from Morris, *art. cit.*, p. 47.

[22] *Ibid.*, 17:2.

[23] *Ibid.*, 6:2.

These are the sorts of abuses that provoked the Circum-cellions in Africa, or the massive desertion to the barbarians on the part of Spanish and Gallic provincials.[24] It is interest-ing that Augustine was to protest against the Pelagians' denunciation of wealth (*De Gestis Pelagii*). It shows, how-ever, that some educated Christians were attempting, under the inspiration of religion, to show up and if possible cure the social evils of the day. If justice was demanded of a Christian on earth, how much more would it be in heaven?

Behind this drive for practical reform was the belief that a Christian could and should strive for perfection. To fail was to fail in love for Christ and to reject Paul (1 Corinthians 7:7, "For I would that all men were even as myself.") There were degrees of sinning, but no neat division into "mortal" and "venial" sins. All transgressions were sins, to be accounted for by the sinner at the last day. This led to two other important propositions:

(a) The rejection of "grace" (*gratia*) in the sense of "grace and favour." Christ could not be bribed or interceded with at the Judgment. Each sinner had to stand before Him and account for his deeds, against the measure of the Gospels and Epistles.[25]

(b) There was sympathy with Antiochene theology as represented by Theodore of Mopsuestia (d. 428) and the immigrant to Italy, Rufinus the Syrian (d. circa 409). The Antiochenes emphasised the humanity of Christ and the primacy of His will in harmonising that nature with the divine nature. Humans could follow this example and be saved.[26] In addition, in discussing

[24]For the Circumcellions, see above p. 108. For the Bagaudae and their prefer-ence for the barbarian invaders as against the Roman administration in Gaul, see Salvian, *On the Governance of God*, ed. C. M. Sanford (New York, 1930), v:5:20, and compare Paulus Orosius, *Historia adversus Paganos*, (ed. C. Zangemeister, *CSEL* 5), vii:32.

[25]See J. N. L. Myres, *art. cit.*, p. 28, citing the Pelagian letter *De malis doctoribus et operibus fidei*.

[26]For the influence of the Antiochene school of Pelagius, see de Plinval, *op. cit.*, pp. 133-134, 283, 345-346. Julian of Eclanum was received hospitably by Theodore of Mopsuestia in 421.

the Fall, Rufinus had denied any transmission of Original Sin. The fault was Adam's alone.[27]

None of these views was heretical, and, indeed, they were calculated to inspire that section of the Roman aristocracy that desired to practice true Christianity and those who were conscious of the massive inequalities of wealth and poverty around them, but had been repelled by Jerome's intemperances. Pelagius' view, expressed in his *Letter to Celantia*, that the pursuit of asceticism must imply no disparagement of marriage and must find a middle way between Jovinian and Jerome, was especially welcome.[28] In addition, Pelagius' ideas found a response in areas such as south Italy and Sicily where these same senatorial landowners administered their properties with some regard for the traditional virtues and care for their tenants that their pagan ancestors had shown. The ideal, too, of Christian "care" and "restraint" harkened back to the age of Stoic virtues.[29] The continuity between Stoicism and Pelagianism can hardly be denied. No wonder that these rather than Jerome's views were acceptable, and Pelagius' adherents in Rome included at this time members of the Anician clan, Pinianus and his wife Melania, the virgin Demetrias and her mother Juliana and grandmother Proba, and the deacon Xystus (later Pope Xystus III).[30] In south Italy, the family of Bishop Memor of Eclanum was sincerely attached to him, and Paulinus of Nola could be counted among his friends.[31] On the northern shores of the Mediterranean Christianity was succeeding in building on the pagan past and maintaining thereby the

[27]Rufinus, *Liber de Fide*. See G. Bonner, *Augustine and Modern Research on Pelagianism*, 1970 Saint Augustine Lecture at Villanova University (Philadelphia, 1972), p. 20.

[28]The letter to Celantia is published as Jerome, *Letter* 148, in *CSEL* 56 — a rousing moral treatise but completely different in direction and spirit from Jerome's exhortations.

[29]Though Pelagius himself distinguishes carefully between his teaching and that of the Stoics; see *Letter* to Celantia 6.

[30]See P. R. L. Brown, "Pelagius and His Supporters," p. 185 of *Religion and Society*.

[31]*Ibid.*

continuity between imperial Rome and the newly victorious faith.

Unfortunately, all this was to be undone by events taking place on the opposite shore of the Mediterranean in North Africa. There, Augustine's star was rising. His views were increasingly heard at the court of Honorius at Ravenna and his influence was eventually to be as damaging to Pelagianism as it was to Donatism. All his adult life, Augustine had wrestled with the problem of evil and the associated problems of free-will and grace. At first the stark dualism between Good and Evil propounded by the Manichees attracted him, and in 373, about a year after he had begun to study at Carthage, he became a Manichaean "Hearer."[32] He was never quite satisfied. He found he "could not progress"[33] in Manichaeism. He was deeply disappointed with his encounter with the Manichaean leader in North Africa, Faustus of Milevis, a plain-spoken but non-philosophical individual who had found in Manichaeism a release from the outworn traditions of North African paganism. But Augustine wanted more; yet to have penetrated deeper into Manichaean lore and teaching would have involved him in taking on the status and responsibilities of a Manichaean "Elect" with its obligations of celibacy, inactivity, and abstinence from work. This Augustine was not prepared to do.

In his years of revulsion from Manichaeism, from 385 to 395, he had moved in the opposite direction, asserting that sin was the result of fault of will and not fault of nature. At this stage, he would have agreed with Pelagius. One example of this phase of his thought is taken from his debate at Hippo with the African Manichee, Fortunatus, in 392. Augustine claimed, "there is no sin unless through one's own will, and hence the reward, because we do right things also by our will" (*Against Fortunatus*, ch. 21).

By the time Augustine came to write the *Confessions* in 396/7, he had come to a different conclusion. There he saw

---

[32] *Confessions* iii:6:10, and for the influence of the problem of evil in propelling him towards Manichaeism, see *On Free Will* 1:2:4.

[33] *Confessions* v:7:13.

himself rescued from successive stages of ineptitude, error and partial truth by divine act. Without God's intervention he would still be wallowing in sin. Next year he received a long list of questions concerning the nature of sin and grace from Ambrose of Milan's successor, Simplicianus.[34] These made Augustine think furiously and the result was decisive. He wrote many years later in the *Retractations* (Bk. 2:1.1), how he "had balanced human free-will and grace, but the grace of God was victorious," and "I was not able to arrive at the truth except on the hypothesis that nothing came from ourselves." "We cannot resist concupiscence without Grace." Man formed part of a "mass of sin."[35]

These were ideas and even phrases that Augustine was to use time and again against Pelagius. His views were hardening by 398, thirteen years before Pelagius appeared in his sights. Even if Pelagius had never left Rome, his teaching would have been vigorously opposed in North Africa. In addition, in combatting the Donatists, Augustine added a further argument to his armoury. The Donatists claimed the right to toleration.[36] Augustine rejected this in a letter he wrote in 405, on the grounds that free will was merely "freedom to err," and to fall into heresy.[37] In this argument he was beginning to associate his view of Grace with the consequences of the Fall.

"What is it that David says," he asks, "except that he was conceived in iniquity, unless it was because he derived his iniquity from Adam!" His argument also involved the mistranslation of the verse in Paul, Romans 5:12, "Death came into the world on account of man (Adam) *in* whom all sinned." Augustine was following the notable commentary

---

[34] *Ad Simplicianum de diversis quaestionibus* 1 quaestio 2:16:22 (*PL* 40:121): "a quo (Adam) in universum genus humanum origo ducitur... una quaedam massa peccationis."

[35] *Retractions* ii:1: "In cuius quaestionis solutione laboratum est quidem pro libero arbitrio voluntatis humanae, sed vicit Dei gratia."

[36] Thus, Petilian of Constantine, cited by Augustine, *Contra Litteras Petiliani* ii:93:214, and ii:94:216. "If you want to be our friends, why do you force us against our will (to join you)?"

[37] *Letter* 105:16.

on the epistle by Hilarius (Ambrosiaster), which also included the remark that "in Adam all sinned as a lump,"[38] and that this transmission of sin to Adam's progeny could presuppose that human souls were derived from their parents, like human bodies.[39]

Arguments about the meaning of the Fall and about Grace were beginning to stir on both sides of the Mediterranean.[40] There were disputes in Rome over Pelagius' view that sinlessness was possible. If so, what part did Grace play? Pelagius would reply that Grace acted like the Spirit that inspired the prophets, and that it was evident that the patriarchs at least attained sinlessness. "Hearts full of scorn and slackness," he was to write to Demetrias in circa 414, were trying to convict God of placing impossible burdens on his creation.[41]

Matters had not, however, come to a head when catastrophe befell Rome and Pelagius fled with thousands of others to North Africa. He was accompanied by a close friend, the lawyer Caelestius. Caelestius was a far more thrusting character and not too careful in what he wrote. While Pelagius moved on to Palestine, leaving Augustine with the same high opinion of his character as he had previously had, Caelestius thought of settling in Carthage and embarking on a clerical career. Before he had taken even preliminary steps, he found himself confronted by a series of propositions by the Milanese deacon Paulinus, who was in Carthage on business connected with the landed interests of his church.[42] In the autumn of 411 Caelestius was summoned before a local Carthaginian synod presided

---

[38]"Ambrosiaster," *In Epist. ad Romanos* 5:12. See J. N. D. Kelly, *Early Christian Doctrines*, p. 354.

[39]*Sermon on Psalm* 50:10(*PL* 36:591) "Nemo nascitur nisi trahens poenam" and so forth.

[40]See Plinval, ch. 4, for the thrust of Pelagius' teaching in Rome. He did not mince matters! On echoes of controversy there see Augustine, *On Original Sin*, ch. 3. (Paulinus' attack on Caelestius' teaching in Rome).

[41]*To Demetrias* 16, in Stevenson, *op. cit.*, p. 219.

[42]For the deacon Paulinus as Caelestius' accuser, see Augustine, *On Original Sin*, ch. 3.

over by Bishop Aurelius and ordered to explain himself.
The propositions complained of were:

(a) Adam was mortal and would have died whether or not
he had sinned.

(b) The sin of Eve hurt Eve alone and not the human race.

(c) That infants are born into the same state as Adam had
been in, before his fall.

(d) Infants, though not baptised, have eternal life, but would
not enter the Kingdom of Heaven.

(e) Since it was not through the sin and death of Eve that the
human race incurred death, so it was not through the
resurrection that it attained life eternal.

(f) The Law and Gospel equally send mankind forward to
the Kingdom of Heaven.

(g) There were sinless beings before the coming of the Lord.[43]

Caelestius had a logical case. If there were sinless beings,
like Enoch, before the coming of Christ, how far was the
Resurrection necessary for human redemption? But in the
early fifth century anyone who denied the Fall and the need
for redemption through Jesus Christ was bound to become
suspect. Caelestius, too, had raised the question that particularly interested the North Africans, how sin was transmitted, and he challenged the ecclesiastical practice of infant
baptism "for the remission of sins." If there were no sins to
remit, why baptise?[44]

He could not have found himself on a worse wicket than
at Carthage:

(a) Both Catholic and Donatist theology was dominated by
ideas of Grace and Predestination (following naturally
from the key questions, "Who belonged to the Church?
Who was saved? Who was outside? What was the nature
of the Church?")

(b) For the last 150 years the question of whether or not
unworthy ministers transmitted sin had been in the centre

---

[43]See G. Bonner, *St. Augustine of Hippo: Life and Controversies* (London,
1963), pp. 321-322, and the text of the proceedings in Carthage in Augustine, *On
Original Sin*, chs. 2-3.

[44]Bonner, *ibid.*

of theological debate. Was there sin by association?

(c) From Tertullian onwards, opinion had tended to accept the idea of the seminal transmission of sin, and hence concupiscence as the supreme result of Adam's fall.

(d) The Holy Spirit was regarded, at least by the Donatist Christians, as being present in the waters of baptism, and any belittlement of the rite would be opposed. Cyprian himself in *Letter* 64:3 had accepted infant baptism precisely on the grounds that it rid the infant of the "contagion" arising from his birth.

Caelestius was challenged directly on this point. "What is the state of unbaptised infants today?" asked Aurelius. "Is it that of Adam before the Fall, or does it carry the guilt of the Fall resulting from Original Sin from which it is born?"[45] Caelestius replied that there were various opinions among Catholics, though he personally supported infant baptism.

It was not enough. So, far from being ordained priest, Caelestius was ordered by Aurelius to retract his views, and on refusal was condemned. He left Africa, went to Ephesus, where the church had none of the scruples of the North Africans, and was accepted there and ordained in 415, the year Augustine faced disaster.[46]

So far Augustine had hardly entered the debate. He was too busy with crushing the Donatists. However, by 413, he was becoming disturbed at reports of what were Caelestius' and Pelagius' opinions. In this first phase of his participation in the debate, he believed that Caelestius asserted:

(a) The relation of mankind to Adam's sin was simply that of imitating a bad example.

(b) He rejected what Augustine believed to be the straightforward interpretation of Romans 5:12.

(c) He adopted a spurious distinction between eternal life, which was ordinary salvation, and the "Kingdom of

---

[45] Augustine, *On Original Sin*, ch. 3.

[46] For Caelestius' career, see article in *D.C.B.* i:589. For his ordination, see the Council of Milevis in 416, *apud* Augustine, *Letter* 176:4.

Heaven" reserved for all baptised Christians who earned this reward.[47]

Augustine rejected these ideas and sent to his friend, the Imperial Tribune Marcellinus, his first anti-Pelagian treatises, *On the Remission of Sins and the Baptism of Infants*, and the more celebrated *On the Spirit and the Letter*. In the first, drawing out the Pauline antithesis between the first and second Adam, he argued that infant baptism was the recognised means of entry into the Kingdom. Inherited sinfulness demanded remedy, and that as a matter of fact no sinless beings had ever existed apart from Christ.[48]

In the *De Spiritu* he argued that justification and freedom from the Law were not due to natural free will nor to divine admonition and precept, but by grace only. Law was necessary to help man in his weakness, yet free will was not annulled. It was implied in the act of faith, and in all acceptable service. It is brought into a sound state by the help of divine energy. Augustine thus sees free will made "efficacious" by divine energy in the deserving, just as he had asserted against the Donatists a decade before that a sacrament though valid in itself needed energising by administration through the Church before it became "efficacious."[49]

In the ensuing controversy both adversaries started from Paul, but both came to Paul by different routes. Pelagius stressed the liberating aspects of the Apostle's theology, Augustine the predestinarian and dualistic. At this stage the argument was polite. Augustine acknowledged Pelagius' sanctity[50] and, perhaps, too, the common friendship with

---

[47]On infant baptism, see Augustine's statement in *On the Merits and Forgiveness of Sins*, book 1 and also *Letter* 157.

[48]Augustine, *Letter* 156 to Hilarius of Syracuse, refuting views very similar to those of Caelestius, that were circulating there, and also radical opinions concerning the wealthy.

[49]Augustine, *Letter* 61:2: "Nihil tamen proderat quando caritas non erat."

[50]Augustine, *De Peccatorum Meritis* 3:1: "...sancti viri (Pelagius) ut audio, et non parvo provectu Christiani."

Paulinus of Nola, Pinianus, and Melania restrained him.[51] Only in 415 does Augustine appear to detect the heresiarch in Pelagius. As age advanced he fell increasingly into positions he had once held thirty years before as a Manichee in his zeal to show how Man had become so irredeemably tainted by Adam's sin that he was now sinful by nature rather than by will. Moreover, the seat of sin lay in sexual desire, where Adam himself had sinned.[52] In addition, politics, ecclesiastic and secular, were to play their part in forcing decisions.

In 415 Pelagius was in Palestine. There he and Jerome renewed their old enmities. Pelagius criticised Jerome's *Commentary on Ephesians* as "Origenist," and Jerome retorted that Pelagius was "a corpulent dog... weighed down with Scotch (=Irish) porridge."[53] Protected, however, by John, bishop of Jerusalem, Pelagius was not molested, and it was probably at this time that he wrote the most famous of his extant letters, that *To the Virgin Demetrias.* Here he affirmed the primacy of the will in the struggle towards perfection. "We mortals say, 'It is hard, it is difficult. We can't. We are but men encompassed by the frailty of flesh.' What blind folly. What rash profanity. . . . No precept was impossible. No one knows better the measure of our strength than He who gave us strength. God could not command the impossible. What men need is not power but will."[54]

This was fine, manly stuff. It did not please Jerome, who feared that Pelagius' claim that individuals could be sinless could be quoted by Origenist monks against him. These Palestinian monks were asserting that through practising

---

[51]Typical is the long letter to Paulinus of Nola, *Letter* 186. Punches were pulled "Nam et nos non solum dilesimus (Pelgium), sed aliter nunc diligimus" (*Letter* 186:1). For the timing of Augustine's declaration of hostility against Pelagius himself, see R. F. Evans, *op. cit.,* p. 70, that is, "at that point in the year 415 when Augustine writes *On Nature and Grace* in response to Pelagius' work *On Nature.*

[52]Examples from Augustine's writings quoted by P. R. L. Brown, *Augustine of Hippo,* p. 388, to which work I am much indebted in this lecture.

[53]Jerome, *Praefatio in Comment. in Ieremiah* iii (*PL* 24, 787).

[54]*Letter* to Demetrias — cited from Stevenson, *op. cit.,* p. 219.

asceticism they could attain a state superior to their moods and passions.[55] Jerome repudiated these views as vehemently as he did the monks.

The two arguments were going on in areas separated by more than a thousand miles of sea. They were brought together by a chance event. Early in 415 a Spanish presbyter, Paulus Orosius, arrived at Hippo to discuss with Augustine the growing influence of Priscillianism in his native country.[56] Augustine took to him and found him a valuable propagandist against paganism. No sooner had Orosius finished his seven books of *History Against The Pagans*,[57] when Augustine packed him off to Bethlehem to try to secure relics of Saint Stephen for future use in Africa against the Donatists and also to form a much desired personal link between Augustine and Jerome.

Orosius entered the controversy with zest. As Bonner indicates, the diocesan synod assembled by John of Jerusalem on 30 July 415 was a decisive event in the history of the Pelagian controversy.[58] Orosius brought the latest issues into the open, linking Pelagius and Caelestius as joint authors of heresy and including in their "crimes" the more extreme social teaching of the Sicilian Briton(?) and his friends.[59]

Pelagius, however, was on friendly ground. The synod refused to condemn him, and at the end of the year he secured an even greater triumph at the synod of Diospolis (Lydda-Lod) on 20 December 415. At the cost of disowning mildly some of Caelestius' more forthright opinions and accepting that God's help was necessary for each and every one of an individual's righteous acts, he won complete acquittal and exoneration.[60] It was now the North African

---

[55]Jerome, *Letter* 133, and *Comment. in Ieremiah* iii.

[56]Thus, Augustine, *Letter* 169:4:13. He was also concerned about Origen's opinions.

[57]Dedicated to Augustine and finished during 415 — remarkably rapid work!

[58]G. Bonner, *Augustine and Modern Research on Pelagianism*, p. 44.

[59]Augustine, *On the Proceedings with Pelagius*, xi:23-24 (charges repeated at the Council of Diospolis).

[60]Augustine, *Letters* 172 and 179, and *Letter* 4 of those edited by J. Divjak, *CSEL* 88. Also, *De Gestis cum Pelagio* 1:1 and 19:45.

teaching on Original Sin that was under judgment.

It was at this moment of crisis that the superb organisation of the North African Catholics allied to Augustine's energy proved decisive. Orosius returned discomfited theologically but with the bones of Saint Stephen. Almost at once two African councils, at Milevis and Carthage (27 June 416) condemned Pelagius anew. In desperation — for thus it was — the Africans invoked the aid of the Papacy. After months of waiting, Innocent I (401-417) agreed in January 417 that Pelagius' views were contrary to the use of prayer and the baptism of infants.[61] Augustine heaved a sigh of relief. Action, pitiless action, could now be taken against Pelagius. "For already the decisions of two councils on this question have been sent to the Apostolic See; the replies have also come from there. The case is finished. Would that the error might sometime be finished also" (*Sermon* 131:10).

Causa finita est. But not yet. Within nine weeks Innocent was dead (12 March 417) and his successor, Zosimus (March 417-December 418) had different views. He was impressed by the highmindedness of the Pelagians, and when Caelestius travelled from Ephesus to put his case personally, he came as a presbyter who accepted that children needed baptism for the remission of sins according to the rule of the Church and according to the meaning of the Gospel, but not by reason of inherited original sin (*peccatum ex traduce*) which he considered was "very alien to the sentiment of Catholics."[62] Zosimus accepted this statement and agreed that he was orthodox. The Africans were warned not to listen to prejudiced accounts of Pelagius' views.

Again Augustine and Aurelius rose to the occasion. The former wrote powerful letters to John of Jerusalem[63] and even to so obscure a prelate as Hilary of Narbonne,[64] castigating Pelagius for teaching that "for keeping and fulfilling

[61]Innocent, *Letter* 29, replying to Augustine and his colleagues in Augustine, *Letter* 177. Also, *Letters* 30 and 31.

[62]Cited by Augustine, *De Peccato originali* 6.

[63]Augustine, *Letter* 179.

[64]*Letter* 178.

(God's) commandments, we do not need divine aid," and that "infants did not need to be freed from the contagion of Adam's sin by baptism." The same year saw the *De Gestis Pelagii* composed to refute the Pelagian account of the Council of Diospolis.

The Africans also invoked the aid of the bishoprics of Constantinople and Alexandria. The new Augustinian letters discovered by Johannes Divjak include Augustine's appeals to Atticus of Constantinople and Cyril of Alexandria (*Letters* 4 and 6). He underlined anti-Pelagian arguments, claimed that Pelagius had not changed his views despite his acquittal, and that these views were heretical. He indicated too that he feared a split between East and West if the East failed to condemn Pelagius. He also saw that Cyril received a copy of *De Gestis Pelagii*.

Finally Augustine wrote an immensely long letter to Paulinus of Nola, setting out in detail the anti-Pelagian case. [65] The North Africans were not to be moved. Augustine seems to have realized that the theological tradition of his Church and his own reputation as a theologian were both at stake.

Once more external events intervened in his favour. On 30 March 418 there was a riot in Rome in which the ringleaders were Pelagians. Why we do not know.[65a] Honorius' government at Ravenna took fright — not eight years had passed since Alaric's devastation of the city. The Roman aristocracy rallied to the government. A month later, on 30 April the Pelagians were condemned as factious persons, and Pelagius and Caelestius were denounced. Their views were described as "this subtle heresy considers it a particular mark of low breeding to agree with other people and the balm of outstanding good sense to destroy what is generally approved."[66] As Bonner rightly points out, "With surprising perception the imperial chancery had taken the measure of Pelagianism and high-lighted its fundamental flaw: the self-confident superiority, derived from the aristocratic milieu in

---

[65] *Ep.* 186.   [65a] See P. Brown, *Augustine*, p. 361.

[66] Edict of Honorius addressed to the Praetorian Prefect Palladius; *PL* 48, pp. 379-386, at col. 381.

which it first grew and flourished and carried over into the Christian life."[67]

Pelagius' lack of effective popular support was demonstrated by the sequel. On 1 May 418 yet another great council of the African Catholic Church assembled at Carthage with 214 bishops attending. Nine canons were passed against the Pelagians.[68] So far as was possible the effects of the Council of Diospolis were undone, and conciliar authority bestowed on the doctrine of hereditary guilt. Under pressure from both Ravenna and Carthage, Pope Zosimus wilted. In his *Tractoria*, published in late summer of 418, he demanded acceptance by the local (suburbicarian) episcopate under his direct authority of the proposition that "by baptism infants were delivered from the death brought about by Adam's sin" and of the condemnation of other definable Pelagian views.[69] Eighteen south Italian bishops refused and were deprived of their sees, but this "massacre" produced no appreciable public reaction. Powerful figures individually, the Pelagians lacked the popular touch which Augustine had shown in his country against the Donatists. Paulinus of Nola, who might have played the part of an intermediary, was not a man to stand up to Augustine.[70]

This was the virtual end of Pelagianism as an organised movement in the Western Church. Of Pelagius himself, we hear no more. He probably died in the East circa 420. The controversy that now developed between Augustine and Julian of Eclanum in 418 and lasted for the rest of Augustine's life was a long postscript. Its main practical effects were that the Papacy under Pope Celestine (422-432) hardened its attitude towards the Pelagians, and when Julian and his friends found sympathy from Nestorius, Archbishop of Constantinople (428-431), this fatally compromised Nestorius' position vis-á-vis the Papacy.

[67] Bonner, *Augustine and Modern Research on Pelagianism*, p. 51.

[68] Council at Carthage, 1 May 418 = pp. 220-224 in *Concilia Africae* a. 345-525, ed. C. Munier, *CCSL* 149 (1974), *sub anno*.

[69] See Bonner, *St. Augustine of Hippo: Life and Controversies*, p. 345.

[70] See my opinion in "The Two Worlds of Paulinus of Nola," in *Latin Literature of the Fourth Century*, ed. J. W. Binns (London, 1974), pp. 114-115.

Wearisome in its pettifogging pedantries and details, it was nevertheless the anvil on which Augustinianism was hammered out, with all its consequences for Mediaeval Europe. Julian possessed a thorough knowledge of Aristotelian thought which he combined with a hatred of Manichaeism and a sense of superiority over Carthage and its "Punic rhetor," as he called Augustine,[71] but he was also prolix and tedious and sometimes lapsed into the childish in presenting his arguments. He resented deeply the successful efforts of the Africans to foist their theology of grace on the Western Church as a whole. He stood for simplicity in conduct and rationality in religion. As his own marriage had been touched by *simplicitas*, he believed that this had been the original state of Adam and Eve in the Garden of Eden, a harmless pastoral existence. It would have ended anyhow, for Adam and Eve were created mortal and would have died whether they had sinned or not.[72] Marriage and the engendering of children were not the results of sin but aimed at maintaining the continuance of the human race.[73] Sex and the sexual instinct were in themselves neutral — to be used or abused according to the individual's will and acts. There was no such thing as "some great sin" behind the miseries of the human condition. "It is improbable; it is untrue; it is unjust and impious. It makes it seem as though the Devil were the maker of men. It vitiates and destroys the freedom of will ... by asserting that men are so incapable of virtue that in the wombs of their mothers they are filled with bygone sins."[74] He loved justice and equity. He "did not spare His own Son for us."[75] There was reason in creation which God Himself represented, and a universal force of law in which each man could make his choices. "The righteousness of the righteous shall be upon his own head, and the

[71] Julian of Eclanum, cited by Augustine, *Opus Imperfectum contra Julianum* vi:18, and see i:85 for a challenge to Augustine to prove he was no Manichee.

[72] Julian in *ibid*., vi:12. For his own marriage, blessed by Paulinus of Nola, see Paulinus, *Carmen* xxv, lines 100ff.

[73] Julian in *Op. Imperf.* iii:42.

[74] *Ibid*., iii:67.

[75] *Ibid*., i:49.

wickedness of the wicked man shall be upon himself alone."[76] Augustine had banished "the balm of reason from the Church, so that the opinions of the mob can sail with all flags flying," he wrote to Volusian, Prefect of Rome.[77]

Better understanding of "the mob" and their basic fears was, however, a trump-card in Augustine's hands. He saw Original Sin not only through his mistranslation of Romans 5:12 or even in the key text of John 3:5, but in the actual condition of mankind, its poverty, its ignorance, pain, disease, and liability to natural calamities.[78] All these were the result of Adam's Fall. Thanks to this man had lost his "capacity not to sin."[79] Original sin, too, could be defined through the story of creation in Genesis as sexual passion. "This is the evil of sin in which all men are born."[80] Hence, man was a "mass of perdition waited upon by death," and Augustine only avoided an outright return to a Manichaean position by drawing a fine distinction between a mind resulting from a diseased nature and one "vitiated by nature." In this system unbaptised children would suffer the results of participation in Adam's sin.[81]

Could anyone therefore be saved? Only by divine grace. Augustine felt that he himself had been plucked from damnation by a divine act "of pure mercy" and "illumination" as he had experienced in 386. No pagan (or heretic) could perform a righteous act. "Everything that is not out of faith is sin."[82] Yet the numbers of those predestined to salvation

---

[76] Ezechiel 18:20, cited by Julian, *ibid.*, iii:47.

[77] *Ibid.*, ii:1. See P.Brown, *Augustine*, p. 384.

[78] *Op. Imperf.* i:25 and v:30/ Also, *Contra Julianum* vi:21:67 and *De Civ. Dei* xxi:26:78.

[79] So the long argument in Augustine's *On Man's Perfection in Righteousness*, chs. ii-x, in which man's powerlessness to act sinlessly without the grace of Christ is argued against the views of Caelestius in particular.

[80] Augustine, *Sermo* 151:5; compare *De Nuptiis* 7 and 8.

[81] Augustine, *On the Forgiveness of Sins and Baptism* p. 21.

[82] Augustine, *De Nuptiis* 1:4 (no one but a believer could be chaste) and also *Contra Julianum* iv:27 in replying to Julian's argument that the chastity of pagans was as real as their bodies!

was fixed and limited.[83] Those chosen could not fall. "From these none shall perish, but all are elect" (*De Corona et Gratia* 14). The rest of humanity was predestined to reprobation.

Augustine had knit together many different strands of North African theology into this dreadful pattern, which, thanks to the condemnation of the Pelagians, became the theology of Western Christendom. In Augustinianism, there is the Predestination of the Donatists, the Traducian theory of the dissemination of sin found in Tertullian, elements of his own Manichaeism, and a hard, merciless legalism of the rabbinic heritage of the North African Church. Much of this was seen by a member of the losing side named Praedestinatus as early as 435.[84]

Except for the fall of Rome, Pelagius would never have been condemned. While it is quite uncertain whether his social attitude had any effect on the outlook of the ruling, his fate and the fate of his ideas depended largely on political events. But differing outlooks prevailed among the Christianised Roman aristocracy in the period 380-410. His fate, and the fate of his ideas, depended largely on political events. If it hadn't been for Alaric, Christian Stoicism could have played as great a part in the history of Western Europe as Christian Platonism played in the Greek-speaking East. As it was, the North Africans were able to impose their theology on a divided and demoralised Italian Church — with devastating results for humanity.

How may we sum up? No doubt, Augustine had a sounder psychology than Pelagius. It is obvious that our actions are *not* the result of carefully calculated decisions; there is the element of the irrational, let alone hereditary failings in our nature. The facts of sin, disease, catastrophe in the world are obvious. So, Augustine in arguing for a solidarity of mankind and making that bond of association

---

[83] Augustine, *De Correptione et Gratia* ix:20-21.

[84] Praedestinatus, *De Haeresibus* 90. See H. von Schubert, *Der sogennante Praedestinatus*, TU 24 (1903).

sin was asserting a lasting truth.

But this is not the whole truth about humanity. Pelagius was equally right in asserting the dignity and responsibility of man. Augustine's system, unchecked, would lead to fatalism and indifferent conduct — if one is predestined to hell anyhow, why attempt to reform? What is the use of penance, sorrow for faults, respect for one's neighbour? If there is any relationship between God and man, the encounter must somehow be a two-way movement. There must be free human response that demands love for God and awareness of Him. "We love God because He first loved us."

If the means of producing life are regarded as evil, is not the Creator also evil? Perhaps we should not forget in our lives that God is a loving Father, who sent his Son into the world that we might have life and have it more abundantly.

Source Material

Bonner, G., *Augustine and Modern Research on Pelagianism*. Villanova, Pa., 1972.

—————, *St. Augustine and His Controversies*. London, 1963.

Brown, Peter, *Augustine of Hippo*. London, 1967.

—————, *Religion and Society in the Age of St. Augustine*. London, 1972.

Evans, Robert E., *Pelagius: Inquiries and Reappraisals*. New York, 1968.

Ferguson, John, *Pelagius*. Cambridge, 1956.

Lepelly, C., ed., *Les Lettres de Saint Augustin découvertes par Johannes Divjak*. Paris, 1983.

Morris, John, "Pelagian Literature," *Journal of Theological Studies*, n.s. 16 (1965), pp. 26-60.

Myres, J. N. L., "Pelagius and the End of Roman Rule in Britain," *Journal of Roman Studies* 60 (1960), pp. 21-36.

7

Nestorius

The condemnation of Pelagius was a triumph for the North Africans and their theology over their south Italian and Roman neighbours, the last triumph the North African Church was to enjoy. Within a dozen years of Pope Zosimus' *Tractoria*, the African tribes would have risen in revolt, and the Vandals entered North Africa. African Catholicism apparently collapsed. Augustine's biographer, Possidius, writing circa 435, saw only the churches of Hippo, Constantine, and Carthage standing intact amidst the sea of destruction[1] — a gross exaggeration, but it was to be a century before African Catholicism regained anything like the position it had occupied in the West in the years between the condemnation of Donatism in 412 and the arrival of the Vandals in 429.

The fall of Nestorius was also the outcome of conflicting theological traditions, this time between those of Antioch and Alexandria. To this must be added rivalries between the latter allied to Rome in opposition to the emergent claims of the see of Constantinople for the position of the premier bishopric in the East. Finally, as this dispute developed, personal hostility seems also to have developed between the main protagonists, Cyril of Alexandria, John of Antioch, and Nestorius.

[1]Possidius, *Life of Augustine* 28, *PL* 32, col. 58.

Even more than Carthage and Rome, Antioch and Alexandria represented different interpretations of Christianity. Alexandria was the home of Philo (d. circa 40 A.D.) and the Septuagint, an intellectual centre where leaders of the Jewish community had tried to lay down bridges between themselves and the Greeks.[2] Judaism was presented as a religion of reason. The Old Testament was subjected to the same allegorical interpretation as was applied to the works of Homer by the pagans. In Antioch no such tradition existed. From the little we know of Antiochene Judaism, while accepting Greek philosophy as valuable, it did not allegorise, but applied its lessons for the greater glory of Jewry (compare 4 Maccabees).[3]

As in so much else, Christian traditions continued those of Judaism, but in the new perspective given by Christ's death and resurrection and acceptance of Him as Messiah. Thus, even by the end of the second century, we find different interpretations of Christian truth emerging at Antioch and Alexandria just as they had in the pre-Christian era with Judaism. In Antioch the work of Bishop Theophilus, *Ad Autolycum*, written circa 180, though Christian in form was Hellenistic-Jewish in content. Moses remained "our prophet," one "who delivered the law to the whole world, though especially to the Hebrews." Christianity was represented as a sort of baptised Judaism "further developed in the light of Stoic and rhetorical refinements."[4]

At Alexandria, on the other hand, Clement, whatever his personal hostility to much of paganism, was attempting to present Christianity as a religion to which all Greek philosophy was tending, the "true music of Amphion," as he claimed.[5] Far from emphasising the legalistic side of Christianity, Clement presented it in terms of philosophy in which pagan philosophy had a proper part to play in preparing the

[2]See above, p. 16.

[3]See my discussion of *IV Maccabees* in *Martyrdom and Persecution*, pp. 57-58.

[4]Theophilus, *Ad Autolycum* iii:9, ed. R. M. Grant, Oxford Early Christian Texts (Oxford, 1971), and see Grant's comments in his introduction, pp. xvi-xviii.

[5]*Protrepticus*, i:1, ed. G. Butterworth (Cambridge, Mass., 1953).

mind to receive Christian truth. "For philosophy educated the Greek world as the law did the Hebrews to bring them to Christ. Philosophy therefore is a preparation making ready the way for him who is being perfected by Christ" (*Stromateis* 1:5.28.3). For Clement, Christ was not a second Moses or divine lawgiver, but the Word incarnate, the Wisdom of God and creative force throughout the universe, and he takes from Philo many of his analogies by which he describes the relation of the Word to God the Father.

With Origen, Alexandrian theology developed further along these lines. Origen's main problem was the relationship between God and His Word within the Trinity. Christology was not the decisive issue. But Origen was a great theologian and consequential thinker. He realised when he wrote his *Commentary on John* circa 228-236 that there could be a conflict between John 7:28 and 8:19 (knowledge of the Father) or between Jesus' dispatch of his disciples to buy bread and his miracles of the loaves and fishes.[6] These conflicts could only be resolved if Jesus were speaking sometimes as man and sometimes as God. And what was the situation of the human soul in the Divine Logos? Origen asserted the real humanity of Christ. He envisaged the soul as acting as a medium between God and the flesh,[7] yet for all that, the Word-flesh Christology which he represented made little or no allowance for a human mind or soul in Christ animating his body. The idea of changeability implicit in a human mind in Christ was left for the archheretic Arius to wrestle with.[8]

In the meantime in Antioch a different account of the relations between the divine and human in Christ had been developing. The Christian leaders there took the New Testament literally and did not allegorise it. Mary gave birth to a man, Jesus;[9] she was not the passive receptacle for the

---

[6]See Maurice Wiles, *The Spiritual Gospel* (Cambridge, 1960), p. 113.

[7]Thus, Origen, *De Principiis* ii:6:2-3. See J. Daniélou, *Origene*, p. 259.

[8]See R. M. Gregg and D. M. Groh, *Early Arianism: A View of Salvation* (London, 1981), p. 14.

[9]*Acta Archelai*, 50.

Divine Logos. Jesus was not perfected until the Spirit descended on him at baptism. Even then he remained true man, undergoing real tempations and triumphing over them and enabling man to be saved through his victory and escape.[10]

Unfortunately the chief exponent of the Antiochene standpoint was Paul of Samosata, who became bishop of Antioch in the wake of the Persian capture of that city in 261 and its subsequent surrender to the forces of Queen Zenobia of Palmyra. He served the latter as a high-ranking financial official, and, moreover, "it is quite clear that his character left much to be desired. Eusebius of Caesarea, our main authority for this period, gives him a very bad press, but it is evident that apart from his personal failings he represented a theology that contrasted with that of Alexandria."[11]

Paul separated the Logos or Word and the human Jesus. He believed that Jesus was a man in whom the Spirit had taken up his abode at his baptism "as in a temple" (compare John 2:21) and that the Word therefore was "conjoined to him who came from David."[12] Jesus Christ therefore could be regarded as having been inspired as the prophets of Israel were inspired, only in his case the inspiration was total and permanent.[13] "The unique Lord was in him fundamentally." This view did not satisfy the Alexandrians. It seemed to constrict the nature of Christ's divinity and to fail to provide the quality of love or goodness that could relate (as Origen had done) the Son to the Father in an intelligible relationship. Paul was, moreover, an easy target for their hostility because of his extravagant character. He was condemned at three councils between 264 and 268 and eventually deposed in 272.[14] The Alexandrian view that there was a union of the

[10]*Ibid.*, p. 49.

[11]Eusebius, *H.E.*, vii:30:6-16. On Paul as a significant politician, see Fergus Millar, "Paul of Samosata, Zenobia and Aurelian," *JRS* 61 (1971), pp. 1-17.

[12]See H. de Riedmatten, *Les Actes du procès de Paul de Samosata* (Fribourg en Suisse, 1951), p. 158.

[13]Paul of Samosata, cited from Leontius of Byzantium (sixth century) *De Sectis* iii, *PG* 86. Other texts are cited in Stevenson, *New Eusebius*, 277-79.

[14]On these councils, see Lebreton and J. Zeiller, De la fin du 2e. siècle à la paix constantinienne (Paris, 1947), ch. xiii.

divine and human in Christ and not merely a participation by the human in the divine nature won the day. Yet Paul's accusers had had to admit what the soul was in a human being, the Divine Word was in Jesus. Jesus was therefore not fully human in the accepted sense of the term.[15]

The third century therefore saw the emergence of two rival Christologies in Alexandria and Antioch, respectively, neither of which was entirely satisfactory. The greatest of the prophets was not divine, and a Being without an active human soul could not be human.

The Council of Nicaea in 325 asserted that Christ was "of the same substance as the Father." It did not define how, if that were so, he could be of the same substance as man.

On the whole, the Alexandrian view prevailed. During the Arian controversy, the orthodox and the semi-Arians (Eusebians) were at pains to condemn any Christology that resembled that of Paul of Samosata, which some aspects of Arianism appeared to do.[16] It was not, however, until the 360s that the questions of Christ's relationship to man and his human personality as a separate theological issue were raised, and then the questions came from a theologian of the Alexandrian school, namely Apollinarius of Laodicea.

Apollinarius, despite being bishop of a Syrian see, was an out-and-out Alexandrian, a friend of Athanasius and an abrasive and ebullient character as he. He is important in the background of Nestorius' career, for much of Nestorius' theology was a reaction to that of him and his followers. He wrote tersely and briefly and said exactly what he thought.

He could not tolerate any divorce between God the Son in Heaven and God the Son on earth. The New Testament did not write about two Sons. It tells us of one Mediator, who was both truly God and man.[17] Had Apollinarius stopped

[15]See H. Chadwick's comments in *JTS* n.s. 4 (1953), p. 93, in his review of de Rietmatten's study of Paul of Samosata (n. 12 above).

[16]Thus, at the eastern council circa 345 that compiled the Macrostichos (Creed of the Long Lines) quoted in Socrates, *Hist. Eccl.* ii:19:7-28, at paragraphs 13-17.

[17]For the texts, see H. Lietzmann, *Apollinarius von Laodicea und seine Schule* (Tubingen, 1904; repr. 1968). Also, J. N. D. Kelly, *Early Christian Doctrines*, pp. 288-295, and J. Stevenson, *Creeds, Councils and Controversies*, pp. 95-96.

there, all would have been well, but his logical and exuberant mind was not content. He pressed to its conclusion a notion that had long existed in the minds of Alexandrian theologians. He asserted that the divine spirit of God the Son was substituted in Christ for a human mind, and he left his hearers in no doubt about this.[18]

First he wanted to get rid of the idea of any partnership of two Sons, God joined to a man (Jesus) inside the personality of the Saviour.[19] If there are two Sons, one by nature, the other by adoption, into which is the Christian baptised?[20] "There cannot," he said rightly, "co-exist two minds with opposing wills in one and the same subject" (Fragment 150). The spirit that Christ possessed could not be "just like our earthly spirits" (Fragment 90). A "man-god" was an impossibility (Fragment 91).

The second argument was moral. If the Word became flesh, it still remained the Word and was changeless. But "a human mind is subject to change and is captive to vain imaginings; but He was a divine mind, changeless and heavenly" (*Letter to the Bishops of Diocaesarea* written circa 375). God could not redeem and himself be impure or even liable to impurity.

Thirdly, from this it resulted that the Virgin was also "the bearer of God," that is, *Theotokos*, a term which was to become one of the centers of controversy in the time of Nestorius.[21]

Logical though Apollinarius was, he did not carry conviction. The suggestion that Christ was not "consubstantial with man" in that he lacked the most characteristic element in man's make-up, namely a rational mind that directed his body, was not acceptable. "What he did not assume, he could not redeem." Thus Gregory of Nazianzus (*Letter* 101:7). Apollinarius was condemned at the second ecumeni-

---

[18] *Letter to the Bishops of Diocaesarea* 2; see Lietzmann, p. 256; Stevenson, p. 96.

[19] *He kata meros pistis* pp. 30-31; Lietzmann, p. 178.

[20] Apollinarius, fragment 81; Lietzmann, p. 224.

[21] Apollinarius, *De Unione*; Lietzmann, pp. 185-193. See Aloys Grillmeier, *Christ in Christian Tradition*, tr. J. Bowden (London, 1965), p. 229.

cal council at Constantinople in 381, as well as by a Roman council in 377.[22] In 388 these sanctions were given official blessing by an edict of Theodosius.[23]

It needed more than Gregory's assertions and a decree of a council and even an edict to defeat him. Basically his teaching was what most eastern Christians believed. A vast literature of Apollinarian works grew up, which were fathered on respectable authorities such as Pope Julius (337-352) and Athanasius.[24] These were to have a very considerable effect on theological thinking in the East during the next century. In particular, they were to color the ideas of Cyril of Alexandria and in 449 to secure the vindication of the archimandrite Eutyches against an order of deposition by Flavian, Archbishop of Constantinople, issued in the previous year. The real challenge to Apollinarius, however, came from the revived school of Antiochene theologians, notably from Diodore, Bishop of Tarsus (*floruit* 370-390) and Theodore, Bishop of Mopsuestia in Cilicia (circa 370-428).[25] Diodore insisted on the unity of substance between God and humanity in Christ, but pointed out that this required full mental and moral integrity in the Saviour. Free will, the ability to choose right against wrong, was *the* characteristic of the human mind. Without this faculty Christ could not be fully human, could not experience the full range of human activities.[26]

Theodore was more trenchant. "There is a great difference between us and God," he wrote, "and we ought not to overlook this difference when we are thinking of the divine

[22] *Council of Constantinople*, canon 1, and for Damasus' council, see Sozomen, *H.E.* vi:25:6.

[23] *Codex Theodosianus* xvi:5:14.

[24] A good example is Cyril's use of the Apollinarian *Ad Jovianum*, attributed to Athanasius, in which confession is made of "one incarnate nature of God the Word to be worshipped with his flesh in one worship." (Cited from Stevenson, *Creeds, Councils and Controversies*, p. 96.)

[25] For a discussion of their arguments against Apollinarius, see C. E. Raven, *Apollinarianism* (Cambridge, 1923), pp. 273-297.

[26] Raven, *op. cit.*, pp. 181-183.

nature (of Christ) and the works done by it."[27] The Christological union could not be "according to nature," because such a union would imply a humiliation of the divine. "To say that God indwells anything as substance is more unfitting. For it is necessary that he be somewhere to enclose his substance in those things he is said to indwell and he will be outside everything else. It is absurd to say this of an infinite nature which is everywhere and is confined in no place."[28] The alternative was permanent conjunction "according to a mode of benevolence of the perfect man, Jesus, from the womb itself, "having the same will with him (God) and the same operation. It is not possible to have closer conjunction than this." The uniqueness of Jesus was safeguarded by the concept of Sonship.[29] Christ's human soul adhered to the Word totally, as indeed Origen in his time had asserted.

These two theologies might have coexisted for a long time. Indeed, for nearly fifty years, between 380 and 428, they did. What brought them into conflict was that they became caught up with questions of ecclesiastical precedence involving Constantinople, Alexandria and Rome. The Second Ecumenical Council in 381 had thwarted an Alexandrian attempt to control Constantinople in its own interest and had decided that Constantinople as the centre of government and "New Rome" should have pre-eminence over other bishoprics, saving only honorary precedence to "Old Rome" (Canon 3). This decision corresponded to reality in the East, as Constantinople was already attracting appeals from other centres. The bishops on business with the Imperial court began to form a permanent Home Synod in the capital which could deal with such cases under the

[27]Theodore, *On the Nicene Creed*, ch. 2, Eng. trans. by A. Mingana, *The Christian Faith and the Interpretation of the Nicene Creed* by Theodore of Mopsuestia. Woodbrooke Studies fasc. 10, *Bulletin of John Rylands Library* 16 (1932), pp. 200-318, at f. 232.

[28]Theodore. Compare *Contra Apollinarem* (Fr. 1). Impossible for God to "be born of the Virgin." See Raven, *op. cit.*, p. 294.

[29]"Let us apply our minds to the distinction of natures: He Who assumed is God and only-begotten Son, but the form of a slave, he who was assumed is man," Theodore, *Catechetical Homilies*, 8:13. See Kelly, *Doctrines*, p. 305.

presiding Bishop of Constantinople.[30] But the council's decision offended both Alexandria and Rome gravely. Alexandria prided itself on being the "city of the orthodox" and the city of Athanasius; Rome pointed to the lack of Apostolic foundation at Constantinople, which alone could justify claims to pre-eminence.

In 403, the Alexandrians, supported by some bishops in Asia Minor, made their weight felt through their intrigues against John Chrysostom, Bishop of Constantinople (397-404), and they were instrumental in shaking his position so that his enemies at court could get him exiled. Under his successor, Atticus, Rome and Constantinople were rivals for the ecclesiastical control of the important region of Eastern Illyricum with Thessalonica as its capital, but this went in favor of Constantinople, thanks to the emperor's decision on the significant ground that Constantinople "enjoyed the prerogatives of Old Rome."[31] There was, however, no further open conflict until the appointment of Nestorius as (Arch)Bishop of Constantinople in 428. This could be significant, pointing to the genuineness of Cyril of Alexandria's fears concerning the doctrines being taught at Constantinople and acquitting him of a premeditated attack on the privileges of the capital's bishopric. Nestorius was a monk and presbyter from Antioch and was the personal choice of the emperor Theodosius II (408-450). It was not a good one.

Personally, Nestorius was described by a contemporary, the historian Socrates, as completely lacking in tact, to which he added ignorance of any theological position other than his own and an inability to stop talking.[32]

In his first months in office he made himself thoroughly unpopular in the capital by his harsh treatment of the Arians, Macedonians, and Novatianists, heretics and schismatics certainly, but personally respected citizens. He

---

[30]The Home Synod first comes into notice under Archbishop Nectarius (381-397) and probably owes its formal institution to him.

[31]*Codex Theod.* xvi:2:45 of 14 July 421.

[32]Socrates, *H.E.* vii:32.

roused opposition by repeatedly attacking the term *Theoto-kos* (bearer of God) used popularly to describe the Virgin. Nestorius would concede that she was *Christotokos* (bearer of Christ) but not *Theotokos*. "It was obvious," says Socrates, "that Nestorius had very little acquaintance with the old theologians, men such as Origen and Eusebius, who had discussed the term."[33] Indeed, the monk of Antioch probably ignored them as bearing the stamp of the rival school of theology.

Reports of Nestorius' views reached Cyril, (Arch)Bishop of Alexandria. Cyril had been bishop since 412; he was a tough and unbending character, a brilliant theologian of the Alexandrian school but with more than a fair share of malice and jealousy in his character. In 415 he had connived at the death of the last great Alexandrian Neo-Platonist philosopher, Hypatia.[34] Years before Nestorius arrived on the scene, Cyril argued that the Word was always the same and the Incarnation made no difference to this. The "nature of Christ was always divine." At the Incarnation, He "took on the form of a servant" (Philippians 2:7) by assuming a body. Cyril accepted a formula which he believed to be that of Athanasius but which was in reality Apollinarian, that Christ was "in one nature and that incarnate of the Divine Word." Any suggestion that the humanity of Christ consti-tuted a nature he rejected out of hand.[35]

Nestorius saw matters differently. Following Theodore of Mopsuestia (d. 428), Diodore's successor as the leading theologian of the Antiochene school, he started with the idea that Godhead and manhood were fundamentally dif-ferent, yet both existed in Christ. The union of God and man in Christ was more fundamental than had ever been preached by Paul of Samosata. God "united to Himself the one (that is, Jesus) whom He assumed (at his baptism) in his entirety and prepared him to share with Himself all the

---

[33] *Ibid.*

[34] Implied by Socrates, *H.E.* vii:15.

[35] Cyril, *Paschal Homily*, preached in 421, *PG* 77, pp. 568-572. See H. Chadwick, "Eucharist and Christology in the Nestorian Controversy," *JTS* n.s. 2 (1951), pp. 145-164 at pp.150-152.

honour which the indweller, being Son by nature, enjoys," so that there was a complete sharing of qualities between God and man. There was no adoption into the Godhead as preached by Paul of Samosata and Arius in this. Jesus was never independent of the Word. The means chosen by God for his purpose, namely "good pleasure" (Theodore's phrase), does not translate happily into English, but what Nestorius meant was that the harmony of wills was so complete that manhood and Godhead existed as one in Christ. There was a reciprocal presence of Word and humanity.[36] Augustine would have agreed with this.

For us Westerners, the subsequent quarrel between Cyril and Nestorius may seem to have been over words. In fact, there *is* a difference between regarding Christ as "Word made flesh," starting from his heavenly nature, and the Word "dwelling in a body as His temple" (cf. John 2:21). In the one case Christ is not associated with any particular human being with his load of sins and failings. He remains God, only assuming a body to perform his ministry on earth. In the other, he is associated with a perfect man, Jesus of Nazareth, recorded in Scripture, and raises man by his example toward his destined salvation. He is "high priest" and "great pioneer" of the Letter to the Hebrews. It was a biblical view as opposed to a Platonist view of Christ.

As often happens, it was the presence of non-theological factors that rendered the quarrel irreconcilable. First, some of Cyril's clergy appeared in Constantinople, appealing against the high-handed actions of their bishop. Cyril was not prepared to accept disparagement of his own position. Second, Nestorius allowed some of the Pelagian exiles from south Italy, including Julian of Eclanum, to stay in the capital, thus alienating Pope Celestine. Very quickly the alliance between Rome and Alexandria was revived.

Nestorius' sermons were circulated in Rome and Alexandria. Cyril became angry and alarmed. He asked Nestorius (*Letter* 12 to Nestorius) to accept the current use of the term *Theotokos*. Nestorius was polite but evasive, and he now chose to write to Pope Celestine as a fellow-bishop, asking

---

[36]See Grillmeier, *op. cit.*, pp. 374-379.

why he should refuse communion to the four Pelagian bishops living in Constantinople. He wrote, however, in Greek, of which language Celestine was ignorant, while the latter was also receiving biased accounts of Nestorius' teaching from his agents in the capital. The bias is important because by and large Western theologians accepted the Nestorian or two-nature view of Christ. The humanity and divinity within Christ did act distinctively, Christ hungering, thirsting, weeping and suffering as man, yet healing and rising from the dead immortal as God. So much was to be asserted by Pope Leo in his *Tome* nineteen years later. In addition, the Western doctrine of the Atonement depended on a fully human Saviour whose suffering and death ransomed mankind from the Devil, as did also the reply of Western theologians such as Ambrose to the Arians. Had it not been for disciplinary and personal factors, Rome and the West must have sided with Nestorius.

In February 430 Cyril sent a *Second Letter to Nestorius*.[37] This, definitely hostile and arrogant in tone, reveals the heart of his theology. "We do not say that the nature of the Word was changed and became flesh, nor that He was transformed into a complete human being. I mean one of soul and body; but this rather, that the Word had united to Himself in His own individuality (*hypostasis*) in an ineffable and inconceivable manner, flesh animated with a rational soul, became Man and was called the Son of Man." Thus, every act which the Gospels recorded of Christ as doing, whether ordinary day-to-day tasks or performing miracles, was the act of a single being, God-in-Christ.

The gage had been thrown down, and in the ensuing conflict Cyril showed himself the more able tactician. He outmanoeuvered both Nestorius and the imperial court. He wrote to Pope Celestine in flattering terms and in Latin, and he was rewarded by the decision in August 430 of a Roman synod to condemn Nestorius' teaching and ordering Nestorius to recant within ten days on pain of excommunication.

---

[37]The text of Cyril's Second and Third Letters to Nestorius will be found with commentary in T. H. Bindley and F. W. Green, *Oecumenical Documents of the Faith*, 4th ed. (London, 1950), pp. 87-137.

Cyril was appointed papal commissioner to execute the sentence on behalf of the sees of Rome and Alexandria. Antioch and other important sees were invited to adhere to the same policy. The Antiochenes at this stage could just accept the term *Theotokos* and did not rally immediately to Nestorius.

Cyril, however, over-reached himself. His *Third Letter to Nestorius*, received in Constantinople on 6 December 430, re-stated his theological position and contained a poignant exposition of his Eucharistic doctrine in which the truly divine nature of the elements was stressed with profound veneration, but he added a list of twelve propositions (the Twelve Anathemas) to which he required Nestorius' assent. Some of these statements were obviously Apollinarian in inspiration, such as that (Number 4) that challenged both Antiochene and Western Christologies by condemning those who attributed some of Jesus' recorded acts to his humanity and others to his divinity, and similarly Number 12 that spoke of the Word suffering in the flesh. Support for Nestorius began to increase in Antioch and very quickly Cyril was answered by a statement, probably drafted by Theodoret, Bishop of Cyrrhus, north of Antioch, of twelve Counter-Anathemas setting forth the Antiochene viewpoint. The emperor Theodosius II ignored the Pope's condemnation of Nestorius' views and summoned a council to meet at Ephesus in June 431 to decide the issues, and he sent a layman, the Count Candidian, to preside.

At Ephesus, however, Cyril proved his mastery. He arrived on the scene first. He won the support of the local bishop, Memnon, who aimed at freedom from any interference in his affairs from the capital, and he gained support both from among the bishops of Asia Minor, more than 200 of whom arrived in the city, and also from the local populace. Without awaiting the arrival of John of Antioch, Cyril had himself elected president of the council as well as chief accuser, and he persuaded the 200 or so bishops who were there already to condemn Nestorius. Faced with the deceptively simple question, did the doctrine of Nestorius or Cyril accord best with the Creed of Nicaea, the bishops voted unanimously in favour of Cyril. In the evening of 22 June

431, Nestorius was condemned as "the new Judas" and deprived of his bishopric and all priestly dignities. The sentence was received with rapture by the population of Ephesus. "Mary has triumphed over Nestorius," they chanted; and Cyril sent an esctatic letter recounting his triumph to his congregation in Alexandria (*Letter* 24).[38]

On 26 June John of Antioch at last arrived and he promptly assembled a council of 68 bishops which excommunicated Cyril on the same ground as he had had Nestorius condemned, namely that his teaching constituted an addition to the Creed of Nicaea. There followed a month of furious intrigues in whicn Cyril's lavish bribes, plus the support of the Papal legates who arrived at Ephesus on 10 July, turned the scales against Nestorius. Theodosius II withdrew his support from his archbishop. Perhaps he sensed the tide of popular feeling running in the opposite direction and, ever observant of this factor, he decided that Nestorius would have to go. It was, moreover, essential to retain the unswerving loyalty of the bishops of Asia Minor if the see of Constantinople was to prosper in the future and this Nestorius had failed to achieve.

Nestorius was therefore sacrificed and sent into exile. *Theotokos* was accepted as the orthodox term for the Virgin, but Cyril's *Twelve Anathemas* were not accepted, and Theodosius told the archbishops of Alexandria and Antioch to compose their differences or face punishment. They took the hint and in April 433 agreed to a Formula of Reunion.[39] This entrenched the acknowledgement of the incarnate Christ "in two natures" and agreed that the question of "one" or "two" natures had been a matter of disagreement among the fathers in the past. Hedged about with qualifications, the new definition fell just within Cyril's teaching while outraging some of his more fervent associates, and it also just satisfied the Antiochenes, so much that was agreed upon was destined to form the basis for the Definition of Chalcedon in 451.

[38]Also, *Letter* 20, and Theodoret of Cyrrhus, *Letter* 152.

[39]Cyril, *Letter* 39. For texts and commentary, see Bindley and Green, *op. cit.*, pp. 138-148.

The events leading up to the Formula of Reunion show where power in Church affairs lay. Neither Pope nor archbishop could hope to challenge successfully the expressed preferences of the emperor. The enforcement of peace based on compromise had been due to Theodosius II and in so doing vindicated the ecclesiastical as well as the political position of Constantinople. Nestorius had indeed fallen, but his cause was still alive and the prerogatives of the new see remained intact. Rome found itself relegated to the sidelines, though Pope Xystus III (432-440), now tacking in the direction of Antioch, wrote to remind Bishop John, "You have learnt from the outcome of this affair (the Formula of Reunion) what it means to be like-minded with us."[40] The next crisis of 449 was to show that papal aid would avail those who relied on it precisely nothing if the emperor had already made his mind up the other way.

By this time the dramatis personae were changing; Nestorius' two successors had passed away. At Rome Xystus had given way to Leo. John of Antioch died in 441 and Cyril in 444. The quarrels between supporters and opponents of the rival theologies, however, remained deep and bitter. Hear how an Antiochene, probably Theodoret of Cyrrhus in Syria, commented on the news of Cyril's death. "At last and with difficulty the villain has gone. The good and gentle pass away too soon; the bad prolong with life for years.... This wretch, however, has not been dismissed by the Ruler of our souls like other men, that he may possess for longer time the things which seem too full of joy.... His survivors are indeed delighted at his departure. The dead maybe are sorry." There was fear they might send him back to earth. Therefore, urges the writer, the Archbishop of Antioch should tell the guild of undertakers "to lay a very big, heavy stone on his grave for fear he should come back and show his changeable mind once more. Let him take his new doctrines to the shades below and preach to them all day and all night."[41]

[40]Pope Xystus, *Letter* 6:5, *PL* 50, p. 609A.

[41]The letter circulated under Theodoret's name as *Letter* 180, but was allegedly addressed to John of Antioch who died in 441, three years before Cyril's death. The true addressee may have been John's successor, Domnus.

Nestorius meantime lived on. He survived to see the partial vindication of his views at the Council of Chalcedon in 451. He wrote a personal defence that has survived in a work quaintly called *The Bazaar of Heraclides*.[42] It shows him more mature and noble in adversity than he had been in authority. "God brought not these things on my account," he wrote of Chalcedon, "for who is Nestorius, or what is his life, or what is his death in the world, but because of the truth that God has given unto the world" (*Bazaar*, p. 514). And he concludes, "My dearest wish is that God should be blessed in the heavens and upon earth. As for Nestorius, let him remain anathema."

Source Material

Bethune Baker, J. F., *Nestorius and His Teaching*, Cambridge, 1908.

Chadwick, H., "Eucharist and Christology in the Nestorian Controversy," *JTS*. n.s. 2.2. (1951), 145-164.

Greer, R. A., *Theodore of Mopsuestia, Exegete and Theologian*, Oxford, 1961.

Loofs, F., *Nestorius and His Place in the History of Christian Doctrine*, Cambridge, 1914.

Norris, R. A., *Manhood and Christ: A Study in the Christology of Theodore of Mopsuestia*.

Prestige, G. L., *Fathers and Heretics*, Oxford, 1941.

Raven, C. E., *Apollinarianism*, Cambridge, 1923.

Sellers, R. V., *Two Ancient Christologies*, London, SPCK, 1954.

(There are good chapters on Cyril and Nestorius in all the major textbooks on early Christian history, such as B. J. Kidd, J. Duchesne and A. Grillmeier.)

---

[42]English translation by G. R. Driver and L. Hodgson, Oxford, 1925.

8

Severus of Antioch

Even more than Nestorius, Severus of Antioch (circa 467-538) was a reluctant dissenter. He represented the opposite side in the Christological controversy, that is, he held that the genuine views of Cyril of Alexandria, to which he was devoted, had been overlaid at the Council of Chalcedon. The compromise arrived at there had been designed to conciliate Pope Leo, to destroy the pretensions of Cyril's successor Dioscorus, and to vindicate the see of Constantinople. In so doing, it had come near to sustaining the teaching of Nestorius. The movement in the Eastern provinces of the empire to which Severus was to contribute so much only gradually and reluctantly developed into the Monophysite schism. By the end of the sixth century, however, this had involved regional and particularist movements in Syria and Egypt, as well as the national churches in Armenia, Nubia, and Ethiopia.

We trace briefly the events that led to this situation.[1] The Council of Chalcedon had been summoned by the emperor Marcian (450-457) and his consort Pulcheria (d. 453) to undo the damage caused by Dioscorus at the Second Council of Ephesus in 449. There the overweening arrogance and

[1] For the events, see ch. 1 of my *The Rise of the Monophysite Movement* (Cambridge, 1972 and 1979). I have drawn on this work for much of the material in this chapter.

thrust of the Egyptian patriarch had resulted not only in the acceptance of a One Nature Christology as the empire's orthodoxy, but a veritable "slaughter" of his rivals, the deposition of the Patriarchs of Antioch and Constantinople, the affronting of the Pope's legates, and the ignoring of Leo's views contained in *Tome* of Leo.

The emperor Theodosius II, who had supported Dioscorus and his views, died, however, as the result of an accident on 28 July 450. There was an immediate shift of policy by his successors, the emperor Marcian and the empress Pulcheria, designed above all to restore harmony between Rome and New Rome (Constantinople). The result was the gathering at Chalcedon of the largest assemblage ever brought together by the emperor on a single occasion. The number of participants at the council probably exceeded 520, the number officially claimed. There, between 8 October and 10 November 451, in sixteen long and sometimes turbulent sessions, the assembled bishops argued their points of view regarding the true Definition of the Person of Christ before the emperor or his lay advisors.

The outcome was a compromise, as we have said, by which Cyril's theology, though remaining the touchstone of orthodoxy, was subtly undermined by wording that would have allowed his great rival to be numbered among the saints. The Definition was laid down that Jesus Christ was "born of the Virgin Theotokos as to the manhood, one and the same Christ, Son and Lord, Only-begotten, made known to us in two Natures, unconfusedly, unchangeably, indivisibly, inseparably, the difference of the Natures being in no way removed because of the Union, but rather the properties of each nature being preserved and concurring into one Prosopon and one Hypostasis."[2]

All this sounds, and was intended to be, extremely technical. Nestorius' exile had been accepted by the Antiochenes, but the latter were determined that the Two Nature formula

---

[2]For the text, see E. Schwartz, *Acta Conciliorum Oecumenicorum Tome 2. 1:2*, pp. 129-130. See also the notes on the text in Bindley/ Green, *op. cit.*, pp. 191-199, and the commentary by R. V. Sellers, *The Council of Chalcedon* (London, 1961), pp. 207-208.

should be written into any Definition of the Person of Christ. This was the view also of Pope Leo and had been set out in the *Tome* written in June of 449 in order to shore up the position of Flavian of Constantinople. This had failed, but the *Tome* remained. The emperor's assessors at Chalcedon insisted that its views should find their place in the Definition and the phrase "in two natures... the properties of each being in no way removed because of the Union" represents a victory for Leo, and to a lesser extent for the Antiochene. The four adverbs, "unconfusedly, unchangeably, indivisibly, inseparably," were intended to represent a balance between theological opinions. The first two were designed to confute those like Eutyches who suggested that there had been a mingling of the divine and human so as to make some composite heavenly being whose flesh was not really human; the second pair were designed to exclude the possibility of dividing the two natures so as to make two Christs.

It was a balancing act of great shrewdness. It was just possible to argue that the Definition could be harmonised with Cyril's theology; but only just. The upshot of the Council was satisfaction in Constantinople but a veritable howl of protest not only in Egypt but in Palestine, Syria and parts of Asia Minor. It is important to bear in mind that the resulting riots, however savage, were directed against the Council and its Definition of Faith, not against the emperor. When the emperor intervened and made his opinions known beyond peradventure, open resistance crumbled.[3]

For the next generation opponents of the Definition attempted to persuade successive emperors to accept their view as orthodox. There was no attempt either to establish a separate church or to separate from the empire. This was the method adopted by all the anti-Chalcedonian leaders

---

[3]For the riots and disturbances that followed the news of Chalcedon in Palestine and Egypt, see John Rufus, *Plerophoria*, esp. pp. 22, 25, 27, 38, 39, and 59, ed. F. Nau, *Patrologia Orientalis* 8:1 (Paris, 1912), and Zacharias Rhetor, *Hist. Eccl.* iii:2, ed. E. W. Brooks, *Corpus Scriptorum Christianorum Orientalium* (= *CSCO*), Scriptores Syri iii:5 and 6 (Paris/Louvain, 1919-1924), and Evagrius, *Hist. Eccl.* ii:5.

including Timothy the Cat (*Aeluros*) at Alexandria (d. 477) and Peter the Fuller at Antioch (d. 490).

The theological issue was complicated by the issue of precedence between Rome and Constantinople, as it had been in the previous controversy over Nations. The 28th Canon of Chalcedon had laid down in face of violent opposition from the Roman legates, that New Rome (i.e., Constantinople) should be honoured in ecclesiastical matters next to Old Rome because she is the Imperial city. The idea that ecclesiastical precedence could be ordered on grounds other than ecclesiastical, in this case, Apostolic foundation, was profoundly shocking to the Roman See, and its views had not changed.

However, the Council and the emperor Marcian insisted,[4] and Chalcedon provided Constantinople with its title deeds of supremacy over the other sees in the East, and for this reason no Byzantine emperor could ever denounce Chalcedon. It could be reduced in status but not got rid of.

The period after the Council, 451-482, therefore, saw two unresolved issues: first, that of doctrine in which Rome and Constantinople are on the same side but are opposed by popular movements in Egypt, Palestine and Syria; and second, a bitter quarrel over precedence between Rome and Constantinople. In this Constantinople could rely on the general support of the three other Eastern patriarchates. Both these issues came to a head in the reign of the emperor Zeno (474-491), who in July 482 published the *Henotikon* mainly to conciliate Alexandria.

Zeno went as near as he could to denouncing Chalcedon and upholding the One-Nature Christology of the opponents of Chalcedon in a letter to the clergy, monks, and people of Egypt. The letter, drafted by the patriarch of Constantinople, Acacius, and signed by the emperor, stated:

(a) The faith of Christendom remained that established at Nicaea.

---

[4]See, for Leo's view, Leo, *Epp.* 104, 105, 106; for Marcian's order, see Leo, *Ep.* 110.

(b) Nestorius and Eutyches remained condemned.

(c) Cyril's Twelve Anathemas were canonical.

(d) Jesus Christ was consubstantial with both God and man and "incarnate from the Holy Spirit and Mary the Virgin and Theotokos and was one and not two," "for we say both his miracles and his sufferings which he willingly underwent in the flesh are of one Person."

(e) Any other views expressed anywhere, including at Chalcedon, were anathema.

For the next 37 years Zeno's *Henotikon* remained the official creed of the empire. The four eastern patriarchates were formally in communion with each other, but not Rome. This schism, lasting from 484 to 519, is known as the Acacian schism. This was not the result of Rome's disapproval of the *Henotikon*.[5] It arose out of Acacius' of Constantinople's successful attempt to restore communion with Alexandria on the basis of the *Henotikon*. But the breaking point was disciplinary. The Pope regarded Acacius as a double-crosser for having first denounced the anti-Chalcedonian claimant to the patriarchate of Alexandria, Peter Mongus, as a "son of darkness" and subsequently accepting him as Patriarch. Moral indignation was more important in this case than doctrinal dispute.

The upshot was that for 35 years Rome and Constantinople were out of communion, and the ecclesiastical affairs of the eastern provinces of the empire revolved round the relations between Constantinople, Antioch and Alexandria and Jerusalem. It was in this environment, dominated by the *Henotikon* and the schism with Rome that we turn to Severus of Antioch.

Severus of Antioch was born in 467 into a wealthy land-owning family in Pisidia.[6] His was an anti-Nestorian background, for his grandfather had been bishop of Sozopolis

---

[5]See my analysis in ch. iv of *Monophysite Movement*, pp. 181-183, and "Eastern Attitudes to Rome during the Acacian Schism," *Studies in Church History* XIII, ed. D. Baker (Oxford, 1976), pp. 69-81.

[6]See, for Severus' life until he became Patriarch of Antioch, Zacharias Scholasticus, *Vita Severi*, ed. M. A. Kugener, *P.O.* 2:1 (Paris, 1907).

and had been present at Ephesus I, voting for the deposition of Nestorius.

Unlike that of the Western bishops, the tradition in Severus' family was to regard Christianity as the best of philosophies, based on the Bible and the Fathers, but attained through study of secular philosophies. Like Basil of Caesarea before him, Severus was to combine a philosophic background, administrative ability, an ascetic nature and an intense dedication to the particular cause in hand.

His early years gave no sign that he would become a Christian leader, let alone a Monophysite. Not long after the outbreak of the Acacian schism he and his brother went to Alexandria to study grammar and rhetoric as the foundation studies for a public career. It was a time when there was a brief pagan revival.[7] Some enthusiastic Christians brought this to light, but Severus was not among them. Nor was he particularly active as a Christian when he moved to Berytus in 486 to study law. Here black magic and paganism were much active. Attempts to locate the "treasure of Darius" made by an international group of students aided by Christian clergy came to nothing. All Severus' biographer Zacharias the Scholastic can say is that his hero was not involved. Only when in 488 one of the ultra-Christians among the students, Evagrius of Samosata, invited the celebrated ascetic Peter of Iberia to Berytus quite literally to talk to students, did Severus' views begin to change. Up to then he had made clear that the law was for him. "You will not make a monk of me, for I am a student of law, and I love law," he told Evagrius.[8]

Peter of Iberia, however, had an overwhelming effect on him. "This communion I so hold, I so draw nigh, as I draw nigh on it with the highest assurance and fixed mind, when our holy father Peter of Iberia was offering and performing the rational sacrifice."[9] The communion to which Severus

[7]Zacharias Scholasticus, *Vita, f. 19.* See Frend, *Monophysite Movement*, pp. 203-204.

[8]Zacharias, *Vita*, f. 52.

[9]Severus, *Select Letters*, v:11, in *The Sixth Book of Select Letters of Severus, Patriarch of Antioch*, ed. E. W. Brooks (London, 1902-1904).

referred was anti-Chalcedonian. To this cause he now devoted himself. He was baptised, stayed in the anti-Chalcedonian monastery of Romanus near Eleutheropolis in Palestine, was later ordained presbyter and founded his own monastery at Maiuma near the port of Gaza.

There he might have stayed practically unnoticed. The *Henotikon* had been drafted cleverly so as to accommodate most anti-Chalcedonian views, without actually denouncing Chalcedon. For about a decade, 498-508, Severus looked after his monastery undisturbed. In that year, however, the Patriarch of Jerusalem, Elias, seems to have decided to make an all-out effort to bring the monasteries in Jerusalem to a much closer conformity to Chalcedon. Pressure of all sorts was applied. Severus found himself on his way to Constantinople to appeal to the emperor Anastasius against the activities of a certain agitator employed by Elias, named Nephalius.

This brought a fundamental change in his life, for henceforth until his death in 538 he was seldom out of the public eye. He found himself quickly in the emperor Anastasius' (491-518) favour, but this brought him into conflict eventually with the Patriarch Macedonius as well as his more openly Chalcedonian opponents.

In the capital from 508 to 512 Severus showed that he was as opposed to the followers of Apollinarius of Laodicea and the archimandrite Eutyches as he was to the upholders of Chalcedon. He was also critical of the Patriarch of Alexandria, Dioscorus, who had been deposed at the Council of Chalcedon.[10]

His theology was established firmly on the foundation of that of Cyril of Alexandria, including of course, Cyril's Twelve Anathemas, and he accepted the Second Council of Ephesus (the "Robber Synod" of 449) because this upheld the Anathemas and not because it cleared Eutyches. Every word uttered by Cyril, said Severus, should be "canonical" (*Select Letters* 1:9).

If he owed his Christological concepts to Cyril, Severus

[10]See Frend, *Monophysite Movement*, pp. 205-206.

owed his Trinitarian concepts to the Cappadocian Fathers, believing with them that, while the Trinity could not be investigated through human reason, it could be apprehended through Christ. It was evident that each Person of the Trinity possessed all the qualities of the Godhead, though each retaining their individuality.

In controversy with the Chalcedonians in the capital Severus argued that, however defined, Christ was One. Cyril, he argued, never separated the Body that suffered from the Word. In a typical sentence Severus argued "that God, the Unique One, begotten by his Father without beginning...did in the last times for our salvation take flesh of the Holy Spirit and of the Holy Theotokos and ever-Virgin Mary, flesh consubstantial with us, animated by an intelligent and reasoning soul."[11] This last statement put Severus firmly on the anti-Apollinarian side of the fence.

At the same time his hostility to Chalcedon was equally uncompromising. The whole idea of Christ "in two natures" was "a first class contradiction" — "Jewish turpitude," he would say elsewhere. Leo's *Tome* was "full of the blasphemies of Nestorius" and Chalcedon had declared this "orthodox." Therefore, Chalcedon was to be rejected.[12]

Anastasius' policy was the maintenance of the *Henotikon*. Severus gradually pushed him in the direction of interpreting this statement of faith in the sense that it automatically denounced the *Tome* of Leo, and retained Chalcedon only as the formal means of condemning Nestorius and Eutyches.

These tactics brought him into conflict with the Patriarch Macedonius, who objected to the introduction of the words "who was crucified for us" into the *Kyrie eleison*, and who quarreled with Severus on the precise meaning of John 19:34 (the blood flowing from Christ's side). Was this "life-giving" or not? This was important as the text is cited in the

[11]Severus, *Philalethes*, ed. R. Hespel, *CSCO*, Scriptores Syri 69 (Louvain, 1952), p. 107.

[12]Severus, *Liber contra impium grammaticum*, iii, 1:3, ed. J. Lebon, *CSCO*, Script. Syri IV:4, 5 and 6. Compare *Ad Nephalium*, ed. J. Lebon, *CSCO*, Script. Syri IV, 7 (Louvain, 1949), p. 15.

liturgy and could not be susceptible to contradictory meanings. Amid some horrendous court intrigue, Severus' argument prevailed, and Macedonius was deposed and exiled in August 511.[13]

After a year back in Palestine Severus was appointed Patriarch of Antioch in place of Flavian II, also deposed for "Nestorianising ideas" in November 512. His chance had come, though in the same week as the first steps of counter-revolution were appearing in the capital.[14]

The fall of Macedonius and Flavian II ended effectively all hope of the *Henotikon's* being accepted as a final solution to the religious problems of the empire. The issue was now fairly and squarely between supporters and opponents of Chalcedon, which in practice came down to for or against Severus. The six years in which Severus occupied the patriarchate of Antioch, however, showed the impossibility of uniting the empire on an anti-Chalcedonian basis. The revolution of Justin and Justinian came to some extent as a matter of course.

Severus entered his see amid the jubilation of the crowds and was consecrated on 8 November 512. During his tenure as Patriarch he was confronted with two tasks, a. theological, and b. administrative.

a. Severus was determined to demonstrate that the *Henotikon* could not be accepted with Chalcedon, and insisted on his clergy's being "accurate" in their doctrinal views. Anti-Chalcedonianism was evolved from being a firmly held religious idea to the mark of a clearly defined sect opposed to the religion of the capital. Severus was largely responsible for this change.

Why was theology so politically important? Not for nothing did the Christians in the East Roman Empire

[13]For an account of events, see Frend, "The Fall of Macedonius," in *Kerygma und Logos*, Festschrift für Carl Andresen zum *70 Geburtstag*, ed. A. M. Ritter (Göttingen, 1979), pp. 183-195.

[14]The riot against Anastasius that resulted in the withdrawal of the Monophysite addition to the doxology, "who was crucified for us," took place on 6 November 512, two days before Severus' consecration at Antioch; see Evagrius, *H.E.* iii, 44, and note 33 on p. 220 of *Monophysite Movement*.

regard themselves as the "race of Christians," superior by reason of their religion to the barbarians and Persians on their frontiers, and given the task of spreading their religion throughout the world. Not everyone was a religious fanatic, but in such an environment religious categories tended to be applied to a great number of secular themes. Laymen were as much concerned with religious issues as clerics; those issues bulked large in their lives. Many shared the view of Severus himself that accuracy of religious belief was necessary for one's own salvation and for the safety of the empire itself.

Severus had no doubt what accuracy implied. His first sermon at Antioch on 24 November denounced Chalcedon. The heresy of Eutyches had been condemned there, only to uphold the worse impieties of Nestorius. Only by accepting Christ without reserve as in nature One, his flesh, however, sharing the same being (*ousia*) as ours, could death be overcome and man rise to immortality and worship of God. The *Tome* of Leo and Chalcedon had been annulled by the emperor Zeno's *Henotikon*.[15] This interpretation, however, was not that of the emperor. For Severus, any supporters of Chalcedon became "Dyphysites" ("two-nature men"), heretics to be converted to orthodoxy, whose sacraments were not valid. This led him into curious situations. On the one hand, he was adamant that those who accepted his views should not be rebaptised: indeed, they could be received with their orders and carry on as before. On the other hand, he was almost cynical in his attitude towards those who did not agree with him. Concerning one bishop with Chalcedonian views who wished on his death-bed to see Severus, he writes, "I considered it a sin for us to enter upon a contentious and profitless conversation while the man was on the point of giving up the ghost." (*Select Letters* 1:11). Such was not the attitude to win over waverers in his vast diocese, and there were many.

b. These and other problems seem to have taken up an enormous amount of Severus' time. There is evidence for

---

[15]Ed. and trans. by E. Porcher, *Revue de l'Orient chrétien* 19 (1914), pp. 69-78.

about 4,000 letters written by him, a large part connected with the administrative affairs of his diocese. Antioch was in a mess when he took over. The diocese was practically bankrupt. There was neither discipline nor common loyalties and a host of administrative problems that would have taken a lifetime to reform. Severus describes the church of Antioch as "strangled by creditors," "laden with a burden of interest."[16] The revenues had to be spent in supplementing the income of needy suffragans and gifts to churches. His predecessors had supplemented their revenue by accepting simoniacal payments from would-be priests. People were even prepared to pay for the right of wearing clerical dress without any intention of taking orders, and then after a time claiming a stipend for their "rank" (*Select Letters* 1:8).

Some of Severus' clergy were useless, like the bishop of Arca near Tripolis, whom he described as "having no more initiative than an old pack horse." Another did nothing except "for money or under the influence of passion" (*Select Letters* 4:6 and 1:8). Some were criminous. "The devout Julian (a presbyter of Tarsus) tried to make use of deception to make the illustrious Heliodorus an accomplice in his plot by giving him false information." The "devout Julian" was tried by a roving commission of two presbyters sent by Severus. It was too expensive to summon him to Antioch.[17]

The province of Isauria gave him particular difficulty, divided as it was by personal and procedural disputes and doctrinal issues. Severus was as judicious in his administrative decisions as he was downright in his theological opinions. As years went on, opinion hardened and polarised.[18] By 516 he had managed to get rid of all overtly Chalcedonian opposition, including the Patriarch Elias of Jerusalem. The eastern part of the diocese was held by an even more formidable extremist, Philoxenus of Maboug. But the old

[16]Severus, *Select Letters*, 1:9, ed. Brooks, p. 44 and compare 1:17, ed. Brooks, p. 64.

[17]*Select Letters*, 1:40, ed. Brooks, p. 113.

[18]See Frend, "Isauria, Severus of Antioch's Problem-child," in *Festschrift M. Richard*, ed. F. Paschke, *Texte und Untersuchungen* 125 (Berlin, 1981), pp. 209-216.

Greek cities of Syria II were united against Severus, and the monks in Palestine were restive. In Constantinople, the emperor Anastasius was aging, and he was being opposed by pro-Chalcedonian forces in arms under the Gothic general Vitalian.

Severus' position was steadily undermined in 517 by events in Syria and in the capital. The Syrian monks and bishops even appealed to Rome against him.[19] He had denounced "the holy synod of Chalcedon and our blessed father Leo," and they demanded not only his excommunication but also of all those from Nestorius to Acacius who had disturbed the peace of the Church! In the capital a new patriarch was less favourable to him, and the Western, Latin-speaking provinces were moving increasingly towards support of Pope Hormisdas — a master diplomat with a will of iron. People, too, were becoming fed up with Severus' constant harping on "accurate doctrine" and attacks on bishops long ago dead.

On 9 July 518 Anastasius at last died — at the age of 88. His successor was the elderly, Latin-speaking soldier, Justin I. There was an immediate religious revolution. Justin was as enthusiastic a Chalcedonian as Anastasius had been Monophysite. In a matter of weeks policies which had held sway for the previous thirty-five years were swept away. "Four Councils even as there are Four Gospels" became the popular war-cry. Severus did not wait for the inevitable sentence of deposition. He left Antioch secretly on 16 September 518 and arrived in the friendly Monophysite city of Alexandria a fortnight later. He was never to return to Antioch. Any chance the anti-Chalcedonians had of making the religion of the One Incarnate Nature of the Divine Word into the religion of Eastern Christendom disappeared with him.

Severus had twenty years of life before him. For a decade he kept up a constant flow of correspondence and instruction to his supporters. Gradually the differences between

---

[19]For the text of their letter, see *Collectio Avellana*, no. 139, ed. O. Guenther, *CSEL* 35, and for Pope Hormisdas' answer, *ibid.*, no. 140.

Chalcedonians and anti-Chalcedonians hardened into schism. Severus himself said more than once, "Separation for piety's sake is better than vicious concord," and a number of events now combined to bring this about.

First, Severus' supporters insisted on receiving the Eucharist consecrated by an "orthodox," that is, Monophysite, priest, and by no one else. This then led Severus to replace clergy when he could with new ordinations from Alexandria, resulting in two rival hierarchies in the patriarchate of Antioch from circa 525 onwards. Even more important were events in 530. In that year he yielded to demands from the Monophysites in East Syria to establish a formal hierarchy. "At the end of ten years of persecution (that is, 529/530) the faithful who remained in diverse places began to be concerned about ordinations and consulted the faithful bishops; but these latter feared to bring down on themselves even fiercer flames of persecution, and they refused to make ordinations openly, although they made some secretly. Then complaints arose from all sides against the blessed bishops because of the deficiency of clerics; and they wrote and besought the bishops to make ordinations for the faithful, for the matter was urgent."[20]

Severus gave way and the effect was electric. Hundreds of people volunteered for ordination "like a flooded river that had burst its banks."[21] By the end of 531 a Monophysite hierarchy was in being and northern Syria as far as the Roman frontier with Persia was Monophysite, as was Egypt.

Severus excused himself on the grounds of age from attending what proved to be a final conference in 532 organised by Justinian who succeeded his uncle Justin in 527 as emperor. There were three sessions between Chalcedonian and Monophysite representatives. Like most such conferences, this ended inconclusively.

In retrospect, this conference offered probably the last real opportunity for the opposing sides to come together.

[20]John of Ephesus, *Lives of the Eastern Saints*, ed. E. W. Brooks, *P.O.* 18, p. 515.
[21]*Ibid.*, p. 518.

The Chalcedonians had shown that they had a point in that the attitude of the Monophysites toward Eutyches and Dioscorus was at best ambivalent, and it was clear that Dioscorus' council in 449 (Ephesus II) had committed grave injustices.[22] However, when it came to discussing the remedial means taken at Chalcedon, the Monophysites were on firmer ground. Cyril,·they argued, would not have agreed with Chalcedon. While he had accepted that Christ was "out of two natures, one," he had never indicated a belief in "two natures after the union." Moreover, the restoration of the more extreme exponents of Antiochene theology, Ibas of Edessa and Theodoret of Cyrrhus, showed the real temper of Chalcedon.[23] Twenty years later the works of Ibas and Theodoret were both to be anathematised at the Fifth General Council. One wonders if this had been conceded in 533 together with the Theopaschite interpretation of Christ's Passion and death (that is, the belief that "he who suffered in the flesh was one of the Trinity"),[24] a *modus vivendi* could not have been achieved. Schism was far from Severus' mind. Indeed, the Monophysites always regarded their opponents as the true schismatics and disturbers of the framework of the empire. "Two Natures" involved division within the Incarnate Christ and hence within His earthly realm, the empire. One Nature meant unity on earth as well as in heaven.[25]

[22] An account of the conference written by one of the Chalcedonian representatives, Innocentius of Maronia, has survived. The text is in Schwartz, *Acta* 4:ii, pp. 169-184 = Mansi, *Collectio conciliorum* viii, cols. 817-833. The Monophysites were never happy about Eutyches' restoration to communion at the Second Council of Ephesus. Severus, *Ep.* 32, *P.O.* 12:2, pp. 266-267, wrote to his "orthodox brothers" of Tyre that Eutyches had been vindicated rightly at the council, but later "seems to have returned to his vomit"!

[23] See Mansi, viii, cols. 820-821 for this part of the debate.

[24] Theopaschism as a statement of belief emerged in the last confused years of Anastasius' rule, as the views of Scythian monks from the lower Danube area. They combined acceptance of Chalcedon with the assertion that "one of the Trinity suffered in the flesh," that is, that Christ who was born, suffered and died, was *one* of the Trinity. This was compatible with Cyril's Twelfth Anathema and had coincided with the ideas of the Patriarch Proclus of Constantinople (434-448). It could therefore have served as a bridge between the Chalcedonians and Monophysites had the dispute concerned theological belief alone.

[25] Michael the Syrian, *Chronicle*, viii:14, ed. J. B. Chabot (Paris, 1901).

Justinian, though prepared to go a long way to meet the religious views of the Monophysites, was determined not to abandon Chalcedon and risk thereby renewed schism with Rome. From the summer of 533 his gaze was turned firmly westward, and the easy conquest of Vandal North Africa, followed by the invasion of Ostrogothic Italy, demonstrated his aim to re-unite the Eastern and Western halves of the empire politically and ecclesiastically. In this scheme, no further concessions could be made to the Monophysites.

One vital asset the latter did retain at Justinian's court, namely the empress Theodora. Risen from the immigrant lower classes of the capital and reflecting their Monophysite sympathies, she had shown her mettle in the crisis of the Nika riot of January 532 when Justinian was within an ace of losing his throne.[26] She was now at the height of her influence, and this was thrown onto the side of the Monophysites.[27] In the winter of 534/535 she was probably instrumental in persuading Severus to make the journey from Alexandria to the capital, where he was received with honour.[28] His arrival, along with that of two other prominent Syrian Monophysites, strengthened the hand of the opponents of Chalcedon, and when, in June 535, the Patriarch Epiphanius died, Theodora was able to secure a pro-Monophysite, Anthimus of Trebizond, as his successor. During the last six months of 535 it looked as though the Monophysites could succeed, for Severus found no difficulty in being in communion with Anthimus, and both recognised the new Patriarch of Alexandria, Theodosius.[29]

It was not to be, however. The Chalcedonians in Antioch and elsewhere were angry. The fortuitous arrival of Pope Pelagius in Constantinople on a mission from King Theodahad the Ostrogoth in 536 led first to the deposition of

[26]For an account of the riot, see J. B. Bury, *History of the Later Roman Empire*, ii, pp. 39-48.

[27]Note John of Ephesus' account, "Theodora was desirous of furthering everything that would assist the opponents of the synod of Chalcedon," ed. E. W. Brooks, *P.O.* 19, p. 153.

[28]Zacharias Rhetor, *H.E.* ix:15 and 19.

[29]*Ibid.*, "Cum hi tres summi sacerdotes dilectione concordes essent nec fide inter se separentur, Ephraim Antiochiae (Severus' supplanter) agitatus es . . ."

Anthimus and then, in June of that year, a sentence by a Home Synod presided by the new Patriarch of the capital, Menas, condemned Anthimus and Severus as heretics.[30] On 6 August the emperor confirmed the sentence. Anthimus, Severus, and their supporters were banished from the capital. Severus was accused of waging "undeclared war" in setting churches against each other, and possession or copying of his books was forbidden. In pronouncing this ban, Justinian compared him to Nestorius and the anti-Christian philosopher Porphyry.[31]

Severus returned to Alexandria, where he died on 6 February 538. To all appearances his work lay in ruins. Though he had never trusted Justinian,[32] he had accepted his invitation to the capital, and for a few months in 535 and 536 had seen his ideals partially realised through the election of Anthimus as Patriarch. Now all was over, and even in Egypt, so long the bastion of Monophysitism, the Chalcedonian patriarchate had been revived, and the Patriarch Theodosius was in the capital an exile. Pope and emperor had combined to bring this about.

The movement, however, that Severus had led for so long and whose theology he had done so much to inspire and formulate, was not destined to fall to administrative pressures. Within four years of his death, Theodora had launched a successful Monophysite mission to Nobatia, the northernmost of the three Nubian kingdoms, beyond Rome's Egyptian frontiers.[33] In 542 there had begun the great missionary enterprise of James Bar'adai that in the course of thirty-five years carried the Monophysite message the length and breadth of the east Roman provinces and

[30]The sentence of Patriarch Menas against Severus and Peter of Apamea is recorded in Mansi, *Collectio* viii, cols. 1139-1142, and also Schwartz, *Acta Conc. Oec.* iii, p. 181.

[31]Justinian, *Novel* 42.

[32]John of Ephesus, *Lives of Five Patriarchs*, ed. E. W. Brooks, *P.O.* 18, p. 687, "Don't be deceived. In the life of these emperors no means of peace will be found," Severus' reported statement on setting out for the capital in 534/535.

[33]John of Ephesus, *H.E.*, Part iii, iv:6-7, ed. E. W. Brooks, *CSCO*, Script. Syri iii:3 (Paris/Louvain, 1935-1936).

consolidated its hold in northern Syria and on the Persian frontier.[34] The Nobatian mission was a brilliant success and laid the foundation for the Nubian Christian civilisation whose wonders at the cathedrals of Faras and Q'asr Ibrim illustrate the power of the Monophysite bishops and the devotion they inspired.[35]

Severus himself would have regretted these developments. He wanted no rival Monophysite Church to that presided over by the emperor. Once, however, the *Henotikon* had been abandoned, nothing could maintain religious unity within the empire. Rome, Alexandria, and Constantinople all evolved their own understanding of the faith, and none were prepared to give ground. The union of Rome and New Rome on the basis of a common acceptance of Chalcedon was just possible but at the price of the exclusion of all those who had no mind for compromise. Severus, for all his loyalty to the empire and the tradition of Greek-Christian theology, prized theological "accuracy" too greatly to comply. The Syrian Jacobite Church was the result, and it has lasted until our own day.

[34] For James Bar'adai's mission, see John of Ephesus, *Life of James Bar'adai*, ed. E. W. Brooks, *P.O.* 18, pp. 693ff., and Michael the Syrian, *Chron.* IX:29.

[35] See in particular K. Michalowski, *Faras* (Warsaw, 1974), and *Kunst und Geschichte Nubiens in christlicher Zeit*, ed. E. Dinkler (Bongers, 1970)(essays and papers relating to the international excavations of Nubian sites, 1963-1969).

Source Material

Bury, J. B., *A History of the Later Roman Empire*, 2 vols. London, 1923.

Frend, W. H. C., *The Rise of the Monophysite Movement*. Cambridge, 1979.

Greer, R. A., *Theodore of Mopsuestia, Exegete and Theologian*. London, 1969.

Grillmeier, A., *Christ in Christian Tradition*, 2nd. ed., Atlanta, 1975.

Loofs, F., *Nestorius and His Place in the History of Christian Doctrine*. Cambridge, 1914.

Norris, R. A., *Manhood and Christ: A Study in the Theology of Theodore of Mopsuestia*. Oxford, 1963.

Prestige, G. L., *Fathers and Heretics*. London, 1940.

Sellers, R. V., *The Council of Chalcedon*. London, 1961.

Wiles, M. F., *The Spiritual Gospel*. Cambridge, 1960.

Conclusion

What lessons can we draw at the end of this brief study? First, that the differences between Christians ran deep and had deep roots in history, extending in some cases to the period before the life of Christ Himself. The issues of the gathered community against the universal Church, between the priestly and the prophetic, and even between the religion of town and countryside respectively are as old as the Books of Kings and Samuel. Some of our notable Sinners, Marcion, Donatus, Pelagius, and Severus, represented the ideal of the gathered Church that put integrity and accuracy of belief, as Severus liked to say, above all else. It was an exclusive view of salvation, but is it completely without relevance today? Are all the trumps in the hands of Irenaeus, Augustine, and Justinian? So, too, we find the settled and perhaps, one may say, complacent episcopal Christianity of the churches in late second-century Asia Minor shaken by the prophetic zeal of the Montanist prophets. Interpretations of the faith in town and countryside did not agree. The long-lasting character of both Montanism and Donatism should warn the student against ignoring non-theological aspects of religious division.

The second point, I have tried to demonstrate, concerns the nature of the evidence. The Christians of the early centuries were a many-sided group, drawn like their Jewish counterparts from many walks of Greco-Roman provincial society. To concentrate on one group only, such as the orthodox writers whose works have been preserved in the volumes of J.-P. Migne's *Patrologiae*, is likely to lead the student into a one-sided view of events. Hence, the enormous importance of the flow of archaeological evidence relating to Christianity since the beginning of the century. These discoveries require that all serious study of early Christian origins and history must be interdisciplinary, that is to say, that evidence must be sought from every available source and about every shade of opinion. Working in the field is an essential counterpart to working in a library, just as the study of the literature of the Nag Hammadi library is essential to the study of the age of Irenaeus. "Evidence" is the name of the game, and the trail may lead the student into byways, far from the comfort of a university study.

For the next thirty years or so, as world population continues to expand, the harvest of material remains from Christian antiquity will increase. More areas in the Mediterranean lands will be needed for intensive agriculture or urban development, and further calls will be made for international co-operation to "Save this area or that," following the successful models of "Save Nubia" and "Save Carthage." I hope that we shall be ready for this and willing to see beyond the confines of single disciplines. Now is the time to go out to serve posterity by discovering more of the roots of the past, the Christian civilisation that binds together so much of the world, whether Eastern or Western. Let us do precisely that.

INDEX

*For the Roman see, down to 313, its bishops are called "Bishop of Rome" and after 313, "Pope." The bishops of Constantinople, Alexandria and Antioch are known as "bishops" before c. 400, "archbishop" before the Council of Chalcedon in 451, and thereafter, "Patriarch." The Bishop of Jerusalem is recognized as "Patriarch" after 451.